THE POCKET GUIDE TO
MINNESOTA PLACE NAMES

The POCKET GUIDE to

MINNESOTA

PLACE NAMES

The Stories Behind
1,200 Places
in the
North Star State

Compiled by

MICHAEL FEDO

Minnesota Historical Society Press

Publication of this book was supported in part by the Elmer L. and Eleanor J. Andersen Publications Endowment Fund of the Minnesota Historical Society.

www.mnhs.org/mhspress

Printed in Canada

10 9 8 7 6 5 4 3 2 1

♾ The paper used in this publication meets the minimum requirements of the American National Standard for Information Sciences—Permanence for Printed Library materials, ANSI Z39.48-1984.

International Standard Book Number 0-87351-424-6 (paper)

Library of Congress Cataloging-in-Publication Data

Fedo, Michael W.
   The pocket guide to Minnesota place names : the stories behind 1,200 places in the North Star State / Michael Fedo.
      p. cm.
Abridged ed. of: Minnesota place names / Warren Upham. 3rd ed., rev. and enl. 2001.
Includes index.
ISBN 0-87351-424-6 (pbk. : alk. paper)
   1. Names, Geographical—Minnesota.
   2. Minnesota—History, Local.
   I. Upham, Warren, 1850–1934. Minnesota place names.
   II. Title.

F604 F43 2002
917.76'001'4—dc21
2002016540

THE POCKET GUIDE TO MINNESOTA PLACE NAMES

INTRODUCTION

CHICKENTOWN. GLUECK. KIESTER. NIMROD. RED EYE: Minnesota has its share of unusual place names. The sources of these names are varied: some were named with humor, some resulted from misspellings, still others simply commemorate early visitors to the region.

The Pocket Guide to Minnesota Place Names allows readers to explore the origins of names found throughout the state—from the remarkable to the mundane, and everything in between. This edition is abridged from Warren Upham's comprehensive *Minnesota Place Names: A Geographical Encyclopedia,* which was originally published in 1920 and has seen two subsequent printings, most recently in 2001.

Upham's effort to connect Minnesotans with the origins of the state's place names was a labor of love consuming nearly a decade, yet his work poses questions: Why bother with place names? Why are they important and worthy of interest?

Among other things, they tell us who we are, where we came from, whether our forebears were stoic or whimsical, patriotic or even jingoistic, misogynists or humanists, lovers of literature or interested in politics. In naming their places in Minnesota, early settlers revealed something about their character, and they left a heritage that extends beyond historical fact. Contained in a great many of these place names are stories, which take on new meaning as communities celebrate their centennials and bicentennials, demonstrating that who we are as Minnesotans is often deeply rooted in the stories of our places.

Our state received its name from the largest river that lies wholly within its area. Early French explorers called it the St. Pierre River, but the territorial legislature decreed that only aboriginal names should apply to the river, as well as to the territory. The Minnesota River and consequently the state take their name from the Dakota word meaning "sky-tinted water" (*minne,* water, and *sota,* somewhat clouded).

Like other states, Minnesota has a prominent nickname, "The Gopher State." Judge Charles E. Flandrau explained the origins of this sobriquet in his *History of Minnesota,* noting that the beaver, as well as the gopher, was proposed as a mascot. The gopher won out close on the heels of Minnesota's statehood because of a "gopher cartoon" that was published in ridicule of the $5 Million Loan, which the first state legislature approved to encourage railroad construction. The cartoon, featuring the striped gopher common throughout our prairie region, received wide exposure, and the name stuck.

Minnesota is also referred to as "The North Star State," alluding to the motto *L'Etoile du Nord* (Star of the North), chosen by Governor Henry H. Sibley for the state seal in 1858. And the label "The Bread and Butter State" was applied to Minnesota following the 1901 Pan-American Exposition at Buffalo, N.Y., where our farmers exhibited superior wheat, flour, and dairy products.

Warren Upham, the original compiler of Minnesota place name information, was a multi-talented man whose work encompassed archeology, geology, library science, and administration. He amassed his detailed knowledge of Minnesota's landscape while working on the state geological survey from 1879 to 1885, during which he visited fifty counties and covered more than 11,000 miles on foot and horseback. He became superintendent of the Minnesota Historical Society in 1896 and served with the society until his death in 1934.

His comprehensive guide to Minnesota place names contains more than 20,000 entries. Virtually every community (including many that for various reasons were never developed), waterway, and landmark in the state are found in his book, which the *St. Paul Pioneer Press* called "the story of Minnesota and of the families who settled here." *Michigan History* said the work is "Probably the best study of place names done for any state in the Union."

Because of its heft, however, Upham's edition is somewhat awkward as a traveler's reference. His three-pound volume does not easily fit into an automobile glove compartment, making evident the value of a pocket edition for residents and visitors alike.

Upham's guide is an inclusive one: every place name that could be located and recorded is listed. This abridged guide contains all eighty-seven Minnesota counties and county seats, every Minnesota city whose population exceeds 10,000, and a number of entries drawn from those places with unusual names or exceptional origin stories. There are more than 1,200 place names in this edition, but a reader who does not see the origin of a beloved hometown here can find it in the Upham volume.

The entries that make up this pocket guide offer a rich history of how our state was settled. Northern Europeans dominate Minnesota's ethnic mix, but some readers may be surprised to see relatively few places bearing Nordic or Germanic names compared to those commemorating Native Americans, their language, and their culture. Readers will find that Native American designations comprise a plurality of place names, with at least 170 in this volume alone. Because there are few French enclaves in Minnesota, readers may be additionally surprised at the number of names of French origin or translation, mostly owing to early French exploration and fur trading in what is now Minnesota. At the other end of the spectrum, only one site in Minnesota commemorates a person of African ancestry: Bungo, named in honor of an African American descendant of slaves.

Presidents and other political personages of the nineteenth and early twentieth centuries also figured prominently as settlers named sites, and forty-one places in this book are so named. Minnesotans named fifty-seven locations in this guide for foreign towns, most often the places from which early settlers migrated. These pages list thirty-one communities named for Civil War veterans, including one city, Breckenridge, that commemorates a Confederate general, John C. Breckenridge. The town was organized prior to the Civil War, however, and Breckenridge was likely honored for his service as a congressman and as U.S. vice president rather than for his allegiance to the South.

Some might regard the nineteenth century as the domain of male chauvinists, and they may be surprised to see that in this book more than thirty cities and townships bear women's names. Most of these were wives or daughters of platters and early settlers. However, a number of women commemorated in this way held the postmaster positions usually reserved for men.

Without access to mass media, nineteenth-century Minnesotans were a literate lot, naming twenty-seven towns or villages for popular authors or characters from their novels and poems, including seven from Henry W. Longfellow's epic *The Song of Hiawatha*. Modern-day Minnesotans probably have little knowledge of mythology springing from Greek, Roman, or Norse cultures, but, also associated with our forebears' love of literature, seven towns included here take names from those mythologies. Additionally, the Bible accounts for the names of four cities listed in these pages.

Readers may find that this guide only whets their appetite for place name information. Upham's comprehensive *Minnesota Place Names* is an obvious choice for further exploration, and the full text in a searchable database is available online (http://mnplaces.mnhs.org), with links to a wealth of other sources. The ultimate resource for pinpointing locations is the United States Geological Survey's website (http://geonames.usgs.gov).

Research into the origins of Minnesota place names encourages discoveries beyond the names of locations, offering us an opportunity to learn about industry, art, commerce, education, and more—as well as to have fun. And along the way, we gain connections with a vital essence of our history and our landscape.

THE POCKET GUIDE TO MINNESOTA PLACE NAMES

ABITA lake (Cook County) has the distinction of being the highest lake in Minnesota, 2,048 feet above sea level. The origin of its name is unknown.

ACOMA township (McLeod County) was named by Dr. Vincent P. Kennedy for the Indian pueblo village in western New Mexico.

ACTON township (Meeker County) was named for the village in Ontario, Canada, the previous home of early settlers.

ADA city (Norman County) is the county seat and was named in honor of Ada Nelson Fisher, who died at age six in 1880. She was the daughter of William H. Fisher, an attorney and superintendent of the St. Paul and Pacific Railroad.

ADAMS city and township (Mower County) were named in honor of John Adams and his son, John Quincy Adams, second and sixth U.S. presidents, respectively.

ADRIAN city (Nobles County) was named in honor of Adrian Iselin, mother of Adrian C. Iselin, one of the directors of the St. Paul and Sioux City Railroad. Perhaps Adrian C. also had his own immortality in mind when he selected the place name.

AFTON city and township (Washington County) were named for the Robert Burns poem "Afton Water."

AGASSIZ township (Lac qui Parle County) was named for the glacial Lake Agassiz, which honors Swiss scientist

Jean Louis Rudolphe Agassiz. Explorers and geologists determined that this lake, located in the basin of the Red River and Lake Winnipeg, was produced in the closing stage of the glacial period by the dam of the continental ice sheet. At 110,000 square miles, the lake's area exceeded that of the state of Minnesota and was greater than the combined areas of the five Great Lakes.

AH-GWAH-CHING village (Cass County) has a name that means "outside" in Ojibwe, describing a form of treatment used at the tuberculosis hospital located here.

AITKIN COUNTY and city and township are named for William A. Aitkin, who operated the Fond du Lac department of the American Fur Company under John Jacob Astor beginning in 1831. The glacial lake, located in the Mississippi River valley and extending fifty miles with a depth of not more than twenty feet, was also named for him. The city is the county seat.

AKELEY township (Hubbard County) was named in honor of Healy C. Akeley, a sawmill operator here.

ALBANY city and township (Stearns County) share their name with the capital of New York and localities in seventeen other states.

ALBERT LEA city and township (Freeborn County) take the name of the large adjoining lake, which explorer Joseph Nicollet gave in honor of Lt. Albert M. Lea, who mapped streams and lakes in the county in 1835. The city is the county seat.

ALEXANDRIA city and township (Douglas County) were named in honor of Alexander Kinkead. He and his brother William were its first settlers, arriving from Maryland. The city is the county seat.

ALLIANCE township (Clay County) was named for the Farmers' Alliance, a prominent late-nineteenth-century political party that advocated a populist agenda.

ALMELUND village (Chisago County) has a name that means "Elm Valley" in Swedish.

ALTA VISTA township (Lincoln County) sits 300 to 600 feet above the Minnesota River, and its name means "high view."

ALVARADO city (Marshall County) was named by a railroad construction crew for a seaport and river in Mexico near Vera Cruz.

AMHERST township (Fillmore County) was named by pioneer settler E. P. Eddy in honor of the town in Lorain County, Ohio, where his wife was born. *See also* Stringtown

AMOR township (Otter Tail County) has a Latin name meaning "love," adopted by the town's Norwegian settlers in honor of Cupid, the god of love in ancient Roman mythology.

ANDOVER city (Anoka County) probably takes its name from Andover, Mass., although a local story tells of a steam engine tipping into a nearby swamp and a witness's report concluding, "and over and over it went," thereby coining the city's name. A township (Polk County) also shares this name.

ANGLE township (Lake of the Woods County) received this name because it is bounded on the north by Angle Inlet on Lake of the Woods. The inlet leads to the Northwest Angle, or the "most northwestern point" described in treaties defining the border between the United States and Canada.

ANN LAKE township (Kanabec County) was named for its lake and the Ann River, which commemorate an Ojibwe woman who once lived beside the lake.

ANNANDALE city (Wright County) was likely named for the Annan River and the seaport of Annan in southern Scotland. Or its name might honor the showgirl Lizzie Annandale, a minor celebrity during the late nineteenth century.

ANOKA COUNTY takes its name from the city of Anoka, also the county seat. It is a Dakota word meaning "on both sides": the city is laid out on both sides of the Rum River.

APPLE VALLEY city (Dakota County) was named by its developer for Apple Valley, Calif., the Minnesota River valley, and the apple trees planted at each home.

APPLETON city and township (Swift County) are named for the city in Wisconsin, which commemorates Samuel Appleton, one of the founders of that city's Lawrence University.

ARAGO township (Hubbard County) has a name that commemorates Dominique François Arago, an eminent French physicist and astronomer. Joseph Nicollet originally gave this name to the body of water that is today known as Potato Lake.

ARBUTUS railroad station (St. Louis County) was named for the fragrant spring flower *Epigaea repens,* often called "trailing arbutus" and commonly known in New England as the mayflower. This area is the western end of the flower's geographic range.

THE ARCHES village (Winona County) is named for the large Chicago and Northwestern Railroad's stone-arched creek underpasses.

ARCO city (Lincoln County) was named by railroad officials for the ancient city of Arcola in Italy, but the name was later shortened to avoid confusion with a railroad station in Washington County.

ARDEN HILLS city (Ramsey County) was first developed in the early 1900s when Arden Farms, a hobby dairy farm, was established near Lake Johanna. Incorporated as a city in 1951, the community selected its name for the original farm and for its hilly terrain.

ARENA township (Lac qui Parle County) has a name meaning "sand" in Latin, but settlers from Wisconsin named it for their former home.

ARGYLE city (Marshall County) bears the name of a county in western Scotland, but the city is named for Argyle, Maine, where Judge Solomon G. Comstock, the attorney for the railroad that built the town, was born.

ARLINGTON township (Sibley County) shares its name with locations in twenty-five other states. The town in Virginia traces its name to Arlington House, built by George Washington Park Custis and home to Robert E. Lee, who married Custis's daughter, Mary. Custis named the house for his family's homestead in eastern Virginia.

ARTHUR township (Kanabec County) and lake (Polk County) are named for President Chester A. Arthur.

ARTHYDE village (Aitkin County) was called Millward from 1898 to 1909 but changed to Arthyde in 1909, combining the first names of the Hutchins brothers, Arthur and Clyde, on whose land the town had been built.

ARTICHOKE township (Big Stone County) received its name from Artichoke Lake, which was probably named with a translation of the Dakota word for the edible tuber roots of the Jerusalem artichoke, a species of sunflower. Similarly named is the river (St. Louis County).

ASH CREEK village (Rock County) is near the mouth of the creek named for its ash trees.

ASKOV city (Pine County) was founded by the Danish People's Society in 1906, and its name means "ash wood." Much of the original village had been destroyed by the 1894 Hinckley fire.

ATHENS township (Isanti County) takes its name from the capital of Greece, but there are Athens in Ohio, Maine, Vermont, New York, and fourteen other states. It is likely that early settlers arrived from one or more of those locations and proposed this name.

AUDUBON township and lake (Becker County) received their names in honor of John J. Audubon, the great American ornithologist, celebrated for his drawings of birds.

AURORA city (St. Louis County) and township (Steele County) have a Latin name meaning "the morning."

AUSTIN city and township (Mower County) were named for Austin R. Nichols, the first settler. The city is the county seat.

AVERILL village (Clay County) honors Gen. John T. Averill, who served in the Sixth Minnesota Regiment during the Civil War and later was a state senator and representative.

AVOCA city (Murray County) was named by Archbishop John Ireland, who founded a Catholic colony of immigrant farmers nearby. The name is taken from a river in County Wicklow, Ireland, noted for the picturesque beauty of its valley, called "the sweet vale of Avoca" in a poem by Thomas Moore.

AVON township (Stearns County) shares its name with five rivers in the United Kingdom and with places in fifteen states. Early settlers likely thought of at least one of these places when they chose the name.

B

BABBITT city (St. Louis County) was named for Judge Kurnal R. Babbitt, a New Yorker whose connections to Minnesota are unknown.

BACKUS city (Cass County) was named for Edward W. Backus, president of the International Falls Lumber Company.

BADGER city (Roseau County) and township (Polk County) took their name from the lake and creek, the latter of which flows northwestward and is a tributary to the Roseau River. The lake and creek were named for the burrowing animal common throughout the state.

BADOURA township (Hubbard County) was named for Mary Badoura Mow, a pioneer settler. It is also the name of a princess in *The Arabian Nights*; any connection remains undiscovered.

BAGLEY city (Clearwater County) is the county seat and was named for Sumner C. Bagley, an early area lumberman.

BALATON city (Lyon County) was named for the large, picturesque Lake Balaton in western Hungary. Other origin stories for this town's name suggest that it refers to a railway stockholder named Balaton; that the name is a corruption of Belltown, for David Bell, the town's first merchant; or that indecision over the name led to a "ballot-on" situation.

BALDWIN township (Sherburne County) was named for Francis E. Baldwin, who served as county attorney and state senator.

BALL BLUFF township (Aitkin County) is named in error; it should be Bald Bluff, for the conspicuous hill of this name, which has a "bald" grassy top without trees.

BALL CLUB village (Itasca County) has a name translated from the Ojibwe, for the bat or club used in the game of lacrosse. The bat is a long-handled stick with a webbed pouch used to catch and throw a ball, and the name was suggested by the shape of the nearby lake.

BANCROFT township (Freeborn County) was named in honor of George Bancroft, author of the ten-volume *History of the United States* and founder of the Naval Academy at Annapolis.

BANNING village and state park (Pine County) were named in honor of William L. Banning, a state Civil War veteran who was a contractor in railroad construction.

BANNOCK township (Koochiching County) received this Gaelic name by a vote of its bachelor settlers, for their bannock bread, which is flat and round and baked on a griddle.

BARBER township (Faribault County) was named in honor of Chauncey Barber, a resident of this township, or so the naming commissioners thought. He actually lived in the next township.

BARN BLUFF formation (Goodhue County at Red Wing) is translated from its early French name, *La Grange,* meaning "the barn," which refers to its prominence as a lone, high, and nearly level-crested bluff.

BARNESVILLE township (Clay County) was named for George S. Barnes, a wheat merchant who built grain elevators along the Northern Pacific Railroad route from St. Paul to Tacoma, Wash.

BARRETT city and lake (Grant County) commemorate Gen. Theodore H. Barrett, who after the Civil War owned an extensive farm in Grant and Stevens Counties.

BASHAW township (Brown County) was named for its first settler, a Bohemian named Joseph Baschor. The spelling was changed to make it easier for residents to pronounce.

BATH township (Freeborn County) citizens may be squeaky-clean, but the place actually takes its name from the county seat of Steuben County, N.Y., the hometown of early settler Frederick W. Calkins.

BATTLE brook (Mille Lacs County) is named for a fight between employees of Sumner W. Farnham, a Minneapolis lumberman. The reasons for the "battle" remain unclear.

BATTLE creek (Ramsey County) is named for the battle of Kaposia, fought in 1842 between the Dakota and the Ojibwe. Kaposia was a Dakota village; its name means "light or swift of foot in running."

BATTLE lake (Otter Tail County) and township and river (Beltrami County) are named for an eighteenth-century confrontation pitting fifty Ojibwe against a much greater number of Dakota. More than thirty of the Ojibwe were killed near here.

BATTLE rapids (Sherburne County) received its name from the Ojibwe for two eighteenth-century battles fought with the Dakota on land between the Elk and Mississippi Rivers.

BAUDETTE city and township (Lake of the Woods County) were named for Joseph Baudette, a local trapper during the 1880s. The city is the county seat.

BAXTER township (Crow Wing County) commemorates Luther L. Baxter, a long-time attorney for the Northern Pacific Railroad. He served with the Fourth Minnesota Regiment in the Civil War and was a state senator and representative. Another township (Lac qui Parle County) was named for early resident Hiram A. Baxter.

BAYPORT city (Washington County) was incorporated in 1957. It was formerly known as South Stillwater and originally platted as the village of Baytown.

BEAR creek (Olmsted County) has not been known as a congregation point for bruins; instead the name commemorates Benjamin Bear, a pioneer settler. A township (Clearwater County) is named for its creek, which may or may not refer to the local wildlife.

BEARD post office (Clearwater County) is named for Ole and Daisy Beard, who owned a store here.

BEARDSLEY city (Big Stone County) was named for W. W. Beardsley, who platted the town in 1880.

BEATON village (Kittson County) is said to be named for one of its homesteaders and postmasters, Barney M. Bothum. There is no Beaton in Bothum, or in Barney for that matter. How Beaton came from Barney Bothum is anyone's guess.

BEAULIEU township (Mahnomen County) is named for Henry and John Beaulieu, Civil War veterans who farmed here following the war. They were descended from a French fur trader, Bazille Beaulieu, and his Ojibwe wife, Queen of the Skies.

BEAVER BAY city and township (Lake County) bear the name of the small bay where the Beaver River flows into Lake Superior, named for the animal trapped by the early fur traders.

BEAVER CREEK city and township (Rock County) received this name from the creek, along which beaver and other fur-bearing animals were trapped for many years.

BECKER COUNTY and the city and township (Sherburne County) were named in honor of George L. Becker, a mayor of St. Paul, state senator, and brigadier general on the military staff of Gov. Henry H. Sibley. He was one of three state representatives elected in 1857, but when the state was allowed only two he gracefully stepped down, earning instead a county named in his honor.

BEJOU township (Mahnomen County) received this name, changed in pronunciation and spelling, from the French words *bon jour,* for "good day," a common greeting among fur traders and the Ojibwe.

BELFAST township (Murray County) bears the name of the large seaport in Northern Ireland, possibly given by Irish colonists.

BELGRADE city (Stearns County) and township (Nicollet County) have the name of a village in Kennebec County, Maine, for the ancient city on the River Danube, now the capitol of Serbia.

BELLE PLAINE city and township (Scott County) have a French name meaning "beautiful plain."

BELLE PRAIRIE city and township (Morrison County) take their name from one given by French fur traders, translated as "beautiful prairie," referring to an area of grassland along the Mississippi River.

BELLINGHAM city (Lac qui Parle County) was named for Charles T. S. Bellingham, patriarch of the large Bellingham family (seven sons, one daughter) who lived in the area.

BELTRAMI COUNTY and city (Polk County) honor Italian Giacomo Costantino Beltrami, who explored the northern sources of the Mississippi River in 1823.

BEMIDJI city and township (Beltrami County) were named for an Ojibwe leader, who took the name of the nearby lake. The Ojibwe name is descriptive of the lake, which has a direct current that divides it into two. The city is the county seat.

BEN WADE township (Pope County) was named in honor of Benjamin F. Wade, a senator from Ohio who was a leader of the anti-slavery movement and a supporter of the Homestead Act of 1862.

BENA city (Cass County) has an Ojibwe name meaning "partridge" or ruffed grouse, a game bird plentiful throughout the wooded areas of the state.

BENSON city and township (Swift County) are named for Ben H. Benson, an early area businessman. The city is the county seat.

BENTON COUNTY and the township and lake (Carver County) were named for Thomas H. Benton, a U.S. senator from Missouri, honored because of his support for homestead law. *See also* Lake Benton

BERNADOTTE township (Nicollet County) was named in honor of Charles XV (1826–72), king of Sweden and Norway, whose grandfather was the French general Jean Baptiste Jules Bernadotte, who became king in 1818 as Charles XIV.

BERNE township (Dodge County) received its name because a number of local families had come from Berne, Switzerland.

BEROUN village (Pine County) was named by Joseph Chalupsky for a location in his native Czechoslovakia, translated as "an official or other important person."

BERTHA city and township (Todd County) commemorate Bertha Ristau, the first white woman to settle here, while the lake (Kandiyohi County) was named by pioneer farmer Even O. Glesne for his daughter.

BETHANY village (Winona County) bears the name of a location in Palestine, chosen for the Bethanian Moravian Church in this settlement.

BETHEL city (Anoka County) has a name that means "House of God," a biblical reference from ancient Palestine, selected by Moses Twitchell, from Bethel, Maine.

BIG LAKE city and township (Sherburne County) take the descriptive name of the lake adjoining the city.

BIG STONE COUNTY and township derive their name from the lake, which extends twenty-six miles in a somewhat crooked course from northwest to southeast. The name is from the Dakota, for outcrops of granite and gneiss located in the Minnesota River valley below the foot of the lake.

BINGHAM LAKE city (Cottonwood County) was named for the nearby lake, which a U.S. surveyor named for Kinsley S. Bingham, a governor of and U.S. senator from Michigan.

BIRCH COOLEY township (Renville County) was named for its small stream, at first known as Birch *Coulée*, the French word for the bed of a stream, and later changed in spelling to match its pronunciation.

BIRCH ISLAND township (Beltrami County) is located on the north side of upper Red Lake and was named for its dense tracts of canoe birch, elm, oak, ash, and basswood trees, which contrasted with the tamarack swamps in the vicinity.

BIRD ISLAND city and township (Renville County) were named for plentiful wild birds that roosted in a grove of large trees surrounded by swampy hollows, like an island.

BISMARCK township (Sibley County) was named by its German settlers in honor of the Prussian statesman Otto von Bismarck, "the creator of German unity."

BIWABIK city and township (St. Louis County) are located on the Mesabi Range and are appropriately named with an Ojibwe word meaning "iron."

BIXBY village (Steele County) was named in honor of John Bixby, a homesteader who arrived here in 1856.

BLACK DOG lake and village (Dakota County) are named for the leader of a Dakota settlement located on the northeast end of the lake.

BLACK DUCK township and **BLACKDUCK** city (Beltrami County) take their names from Black Duck Lake, source of the river of the same name. The name derives from the cormorant species, the name for which means "black" in Ojibwe. *See also* Cormant

BLACK HAMMER township (Houston County) received its name from an exclamation of Knud O. Bergo, an early Norwegian settler, on seeing a prairie bluff blackened by a fire. Black Hammer was also the name of a bluff at his birthplace in Norway. *Hammer,* as a Norwegian word, has the same meaning and spelling as in English. The name was likely suggested both in Norway and here by the shape of the bluff or hill.

BLACK HOOF township (Carlton County) was named with the translation of the Ojibwe name for the creek that flows through to the Nemadji River.

BLAINE city (Anoka County) is named for the township, which in turn commemorates James G. Blaine, a prominent Republican statesman from Maine who served as U.S. senator and secretary of state and was an unsuccessful candidate for president in 1884.

BLAKELEY township (Scott County) was named in honor of Russell Blakeley, a steamboat captain and banking, insurance, and railroad executive.

BLIND lake (Aitkin County) is enclosed by a large swamp and has no outlet, as its name implies.

BLOMKEST city (Kandiyohi County) was originally called Kester, in honor of C. E. Kester, mayor of Hutchinson; however, confusion with the town of Kiester (Faribault County) resulted in the name Kesterville. Then, when the post office began in 1928, it was called Blomkest, a name combining Kester with Blomquist, honoring early settler Ole Blomquist.

BLOOMING GROVE township (Waseca County) was named for its groves surrounded by plum thickets that happened to be in bloom at the time a committee met to select a name.

BLOOMING PRAIRIE township (Steele County) is named for the abundant flowers of this region.

BLOOMINGTON city and township (Hennepin County) received their name from settlers from Bloomington, Ill.

BLUE EARTH COUNTY and the city and township (Faribault County) took the name of the river, for a bluish-green earth found in a layer of the rock bluff of this stream and used by the Sisseton Dakota as a pigment. The city is the county seat.

BLUEBERRY township (Wadena County) contains the river and lake, whose names are translated from the Ojibwe, inspired by the low blueberry bush, common in northern Minnesota.

BOGUS BROOK township (Mille Lacs County) bears the name of the tributary of the Rum River. It is derived from early lumbermen, but the reason for adopting this name, which means "spurious" and originally referred to counterfeit money, is unknown.

BORUP city (Norman County) was named in honor of Charles W. W. Borup, who in 1854 established the state's first banking house, Borup and Oakes in St. Paul.

BOWLUS city (Morrison County) was named by railroad officers, but for whom or what is not known.

BOWSTRING township (Itasca County) takes its name from the lake, which is a translation from the Ojibwe.

BOY LAKE and **BOY RIVER** townships (Cass County) were named for their large and small lakes and river, which are translations of Ojibwe names commemorating three children killed in warfare.

BRADFORD township (Isanti County) was named by Rev. Charles Booth for his former home in Yorkshire, England, while another township (Wilkin County) honors an early owner of lands along the Red River.

BRAINERD city and township (Crow Wing County) were named in honor of Mrs. Ann Eliza (Brainerd) Smith, an author of novels and travel books. During the Civil War, Mrs. Smith was commissioned a lieutenant colonel in the militia for her gallantry in thwarting a rebel raid on St. Albans, Vt., where she lived. The city is the county seat.

BRANCH city and township (Chisago County) are named for their location on the north branch of the Sunrise River. In 1994 the city merged with North Branch and retained the latter's name.

BRATSBERG village (Fillmore County) bears the name of a district in southern Norway, doubtless the former home of settlers.

BRECKENRIDGE city and township (Wilkin County) are named in honor of John C. Breckenridge, who served in Congress and was vice president of the United States from 1857 to 1861 before becoming a general in the Confederate Army. The city is the county seat.

BREEZY POINT city (Crow Wing County) is famous for its many resorts. Some days, its name seems optimistic, however, as breezes are barely noticeable.

BRICKTON village (Mille Lacs County) was named for its many brickyards, which ceased production in 1920 when the nearby supply of clay gave out.

BRIDGIE township (Koochiching County) was named for Bridgie Moore, the first white child born here.

BROCKWAY township and prairie (Stearns County) were at first called Winnebago but then were renamed to honor a local lumberman and farmer.

BROOKLYN CENTER and **BROOKLYN PARK** cities (Hennepin County) were named for the former Michigan home of their settlers. In earlier times these communities were noted for truck farming, but they are now residential suburbs of Minneapolis.

BROOTEN city (Polk and Stearns Counties) was named for one of its Scandinavian farmers, Reier Liabraaten, whose family name became Brooten from that point on.

BROWERVILLE city (Todd County) commemorates Abraham D. Brower, one of the first settlers of the county.

BROWN COUNTY was named in honor of Joseph R. Brown, one of Minnesota's most prominent pioneers. During his varied career he was a drummer boy, soldier,

Indian trader, lumberman, speculator, founder of cities, legislator, politician, editor, and inventor.

BROWNS VALLEY city and township (Traverse County) are named for Joseph R. Brown, namesake of Brown County, who founded this city in 1866–67. This was the first village in the county and originally the county seat. "Valley" is for the valley between Big Stone and Traverse Lakes, and another township (Big Stone County) also carries this name.

BROWNTON city (McLeod County) was named for Charles Brown, a member of Company B of the Fourth Minnesota Regiment during the Civil War.

BRUNO city and township (Pine County) were named in honor of an early hotel owner, but the name may also have been suggested by settlers from Czechoslovakia, for the village of Brno.

BRUNSWICK township (Kanabec County) received its name from a village in Maine, the former home of many of the early lumbermen in the county.

BUFFALO city (Wright County) is the county seat and was named for its lake, honoring not bison in the area but rather the buffalo fish inhabiting its waters.

BUFFALO creek (McLeod County) was named for abundant buffalo bones found throughout the area when the land was first settled and cultivated.

BUFFALO LAKE city (Renville County) was named for the picturesque nearby lake.

BUH township (Morrison County) was named in honor of Joseph F. Buh, an Austrian Catholic priest who was a missionary and pastor in Minnesota for nearly forty years.

BUHL city (St. Louis County) was named in honor of Frank H. Buhl, president of the Sharon Ore Company, which opened the first mines in this locality in the spring of 1900.

BULL MOOSE township (Cass County) was named for the Progressive or "Bull Moose" division of the Republican Party, which supported Theodore Roosevelt as its presidential candidate in 1912.

BUNGO township (Cass County) was named for descendants of an African American slave, Jean Bonga. His family intermarried with the Ojibwe, and their surname changed to Bungo.

BURNS township (Anoka County) was named by James Kelsey, its first treasurer, who likely intended to honor Scottish poet Robert Burns.

BURNSVILLE city and township (Dakota County) were named for their first settlers, William Burns and his family. The original spellings were likely Byrne and Byrnesville.

BURNT OUT lake (Martin County) takes its name from an adjoining bed of burnt peat.

BURR village (Yellow Medicine County) may have a name that offers eloquent comment on winter temperatures, but it was in fact named at the suggestion of a local merchant, Alfred Froberg, because Burr was a family name. Alternatively, the place's namesake may have been Burr Anderson, an early settler.

BUTTERFIELD city and township (Watonwan County) were named for William Butterfield, owner of the town site and its first settler.

BUZZLE township and lake (Beltrami County) were named for an early settler. That is all we know of Buzzle, and all we need to know.

BYRON city (Olmsted County) was named by G. W. Van Dusen, an early grain buyer, for his former home, Port Byron, N.Y. It was first known as Bear Grove for the numerous bears in the region. Other Byrons in the state are a township (Cass County) named for Byron Powell, the first white boy born here, and another township (Waseca County) named for Byron F. Clark, a money-lender who offered affordable rates even during the panic of 1857.

C

CALEDONIA city and township (Houston County) were named with the ancient Roman name for Scotland by Samuel McPhail, perhaps in honor of his family's homeland. The city is the county seat.

CALHOUN lake (Hennepin County) honors John C. Calhoun, statesman from South Carolina who served as secretary of war, secretary of state, and vice president of the United States.

CALUMET city (Itasca County) bears the French name for the ceremonial pipe used by the Indians in making treaties or other solemn engagements.

CAMBRIA township (Blue Earth County) was named by a pioneer homesteader who had come from Cambria, Wis. This was also the ancient Latin name of Wales, the native land of nearly all the early settlers.

CAMBRIDGE city and township (Isanti County) were named by settlers from Maine for the township in the central part of that state. The name originated with the city in England, built on both sides of the River Cam. Similarly, Isanti County has an Oxford Township, also named for a place in Maine, which in turn took its name from the town in England. It is somewhat interesting to note that two communities in Isanti County are named—if indirectly—for prestigious university centers in England. Neither Cambridge nor Oxford here have universities, but Cambridge does have a state hospital and a community college and is also the county seat.

CAMP RELEASE township (Lac qui Parle County) is the site of Camp Release, where the captives taken by the Dakota in the war of 1862 were surrendered to Gen. Henry H. Sibley.

CANBY city and lake (Yellow Medicine County) were named in honor of Edward Richard Sprigg Canby, an army general who served during the Mexican and Civil Wars.

CANISTEO township (Dodge County) was named by its numerous immigrants from the village in Steuben County, N.Y., itself named for a Delaware Indian village, the word meaning "board on the water."

CANNON FALLS city and township (Goodhue County) take their name from the falls on the Cannon River, named by Zebulon Pike in 1806. This name had been changed from the French designation, *Riviere aux Canots* (River of Canoes), for the canoes left near its mouth by natives on expeditions.

CANOSIA township (St. Louis County) was named for a lake crossed by its west line, now known as Pike Lake. The Algonquian word for pike is *kinoje*.

CANTON city (Fillmore County) recalls the city in northeastern Ohio, home to many early settlers. Canton refers to an ancient city in southeastern China. The choice of this name was contended, however, by settlers from Elyria, Ohio, who wanted that name for the new town. Though a popular vote settled the matter in 1858, the Elyrians gave up the battle with great reluctance, and records to 1860 also bear this name for the town.

CARIMONA township and river (Fillmore County) bear the name of a prominent Winnebago (Ho-Chunk) leader who signed seven successive treaties with the United States. His name is translated as "Walking Turtle."

CARLOS city and township (Douglas County) take their name from the beautiful, large, and deep lake, which was named by a settler for a friend back east.

CARLSTON township (Freeborn County) was named in memory of a distinguished Swede, Theodore L. Carlston, who drowned in Freeborn Lake.

CARLTON COUNTY and the city, which is the county seat, were named in honor of Reuben B. Carlton, one of the first settlers in the area. Similarly named was Carlton Peak (Cook County), which has an elevation of 1,526 feet.

CARP village (Lake of the Woods County) was misnamed by a lumber camp cook who saw suckers running up the Rapid River and mistakenly called them carp.

CARROLTON township (Fillmore County) was named in honor of Charles Carrol of Maryland, the last survivor of those who signed the Declaration of Independence.

CARSON township (Cottonwood County) bears the name of the famous frontiersman Christopher "Kit" Carson.

CARVER COUNTY and the city and township were named for Capt. Jonathan Carver, explorer, mapmaker, and author, who commanded a company in the French and Indian War and explored the Minnesota and upper Mississippi Rivers and the shore of Lake Superior.

CASCADE township (Olmsted County) was named for the creek that flows through the south edge of the township, while Cascade River, Cascade Lake, and Little Cascade Lake (Cook County) were named for the waterfalls near the mouth of the river.

CASS COUNTY and the city and adjoining lake commemorate the statesman Lewis Cass, who commanded an 1820 exploration through Lakes Huron and Superior and the upper Mississippi as far as upper Red Cedar Lake. He was also governor of Michigan, a U.S. senator, and twice a presidential cabinet member.

CASTLE DANGER village (Lake County) was named by three Norwegian fishermen, who may have noted the cliffs along the shore resembling a castle or recalled a boat named *Castle* that ran aground here.

CASTLE ROCK township (Dakota County) was named for a well-known landmark, a pillar or tower-like remnant of sandstone rock that stands alone on the prairie in that town. The Dakota called it Standing Rock.

CAT river (Wadena County) was named for the cougars encountered here by early settlers.

CAZENOVIA village (Pipestone County) was named for a town and lake in Madison County, N.Y., the previous home of many farmers who settled here.

CEDAR LAKE township (Scott County) was named for its western lake, which has red cedar trees along its shore.

CENTER CITY city (Chisago County) is the county seat and was named for its central position between Chisago City and Taylors Falls.

CENTERVILLE township (Anoka County) was given this name because of its location between the Mississippi and St. Croix Rivers.

CERRO GORDO township (Lac qui Parle County) has a Spanish name meaning "Big Mountain," as suggested by Col. Samuel McPhail, who participated in the battle of Cerro Gordo during the Mexican War.

CEYLON city (Martin County) has the former name for Sri Lanka and was named at the suggestion of a group of men for the boxes of tea stacked in the general store.

CHAMPLIN township (Hennepin County) was named for Ellen E. Champlin, daughter of Commodore Stephen Champlin, hero of the War of 1812, and wife of John B. Cook, one of the first settlers.

CHANARAMBIE township (Murray County) has a Dakota name meaning "hidden wood," which refers to a grove of trees in its valley that is concealed from any distant view. The early settlers called it Lost Timber.

CHANHASSEN city and township (Carver County) have a name that combines two Dakota words, *chan* for tree and *hassen* for the huckleberry or blueberry, thus signifying "the tree of sweet juice," the sugar maple.

CHASKA city, township, and lake (Carver County) have the name generally given by the Dakota to a first-born male child. The city is the county seat.

CHATFIELD city (Fillmore and Olmsted Counties) and township (Fillmore County) were named for Judge Andrew G. Chatfield, who presided at the first court held at Winona, June 27, 1853.

CHENGWATANA township (Pine County) bears a name formed by combining two Ojibwe words: *jingwak* for pine and *odena* for city. It was the name of a village located near the mouth of Cross Lake that had been a rallying point for Indians and traders.

CHERRY GROVE township (Goodhue County) received its name for a cherry grove located in its center. The village (Fillmore County) is the site of the Cherry Grove Garage, built by Bernard Pietenpol, widely acclaimed for his early airplane designs.

CHICKENTOWN valley (Fillmore County) was named for the chickens found at every home.

CHIEF township and lake (Mahnomen County) were named in honor of *May-sha-ke-ge-shig*, a leader of the Ojibwe on the White Earth Reservation.

CHIMNEY ROCK and **EAGLE ROCKS** formations (Fillmore County) rise to an elevation of 1,085 feet and are craggily eroded forms of limestone caused by slow channeling of the valley by the south branch of the Root River.

CHIPPEWA COUNTY is named for the Chippewa River, which joins the Minnesota River here. The river was named by the Dakota because the country of their enemies, the Ojibwe or Chippewa Indians, extended southwestward to the headwaters of this stream.

CHISAGO COUNTY and city take the name of their largest lake. In its aboriginal form it was *Ki-chi-sago*, from two Ojibwe words: *kichi*, large, and *saga*, fair or lovely.

CHISHOLM city (St. Louis County) was named in honor of Archibald M. Chisholm, a principal explorer of the Mesabi Range.

CHOKIO city (Stevens County) is named with a Dakota word meaning "the middle." The name is accented on the second syllable, as in *Ohio*.

CIRCLE PINES city (Anoka County) was originally a cooperative community, the utopian dream of Valdemar S. Petersen. Founded by the Golden Lake Development Association in 1946, the community soon became known as Circle Pines because of its emblem: two pines symbolizing life and endurance surrounded by a circle representing the world. In 1950, Petersen's dream was deemed unrealistic, and Circle Pines was incorporated as a village.

CLARA CITY city (Chippewa County) was named in honor of Clara Koch, wife of one of the managers for an association from Holland that established colonies in the area.

CLARISSA city (Todd County) was named by its platter George G. Howe, for Clarisse Bischoffsheim, whose husband owned the land on which the town was developed.

CLARK township (Faribault County) honors Clark W. Thompson, the largest landowner of the town and the county, who served as an Indian agent, state legislator, and president of the state agricultural society.

CLAY COUNTY was named for the statesman Henry Clay of Kentucky. Besides serving in numerous elected and appointed political offices, he was a candidate for president and said in a famous 1850 speech, "I would rather be right than be President."

CLEAR GRIT village (Fillmore County) took its name from a successful flour mill operated by John Kaercher, probably in reference to the cleanness of the flour.

CLEARWATER COUNTY and city and township (Wright County) received their name from the river and lake, translated from an Ojibwe name given to show their contrast to muddy or peat-saturated lakes and rivers in the area.

CLEVELAND city and township (Le Sueur County) were named by settlers who came from Cleveland, Ohio, which was named for Gen. Moses Cleaveland, who had surveyed that city.

CLIMAX city (Polk County) is named with an ancient Greek word meaning "a ladder or a stairway," or the highest point attained, chosen here from its use in advertisements for Climax Tobacco.

CLITHERALL city, township, and lake (Otter Tail County) were named for Maj. George B. Clitherall, a registrar of the county's U.S. land office.

CLONTARF city and township (Swift County) were named by Bishop John Ireland for the town near Dublin, Ireland. The Catholic Colonization Bureau chose this site to develop a colony in 1876.

CLOQUET city (Carlton County) shares its name with the river, which was likely named for a fur trader. The name retains the French pronunciation of its last syllable, as in *bouquet*.

CLOTHO village (Todd County) was named for a Greek mythical goddess.

CLOUGH township and lake (Morrison County) were named in honor of David M. Clough, a lumberman and governor of Minnesota.

COHASSET city (Itasca County) received its name from the town on the east coast of Massachusetts. It is an Indian word meaning "fishing promontory," "place of pines," or "young pine trees."

COIN village (Kanabec County) was named during the William Jennings Bryan free silver debate as suggested by postmaster Ole E. Olson.

COKATO city and township (Wright County) have the Dakota name of the largest lake of the township, meaning "at the middle."

COLD SPRING city (Stearns County) was named for the numerous natural mineral springs in its vicinity.

COLERAINE city (Itasca County) bears the name of a township in western Massachusetts, but the name was actually chosen in honor of Thomas F. Cole, who was prominent in the early development of iron mines on the Mesabi Range.

COLFAX township (Kandiyohi County) was named for Schuyler Colfax, vice president of the United States under Ulysses S. Grant.

COLLEGEVILLE township (Stearns County) takes its name from St. John's College, now a university.

COLOGNE city (Carver County) was named by German settlers for the ancient city of Köln on the Rhine River.

COLUMBIA HEIGHTS city (Anoka County) was named by its platter, Thomas Lowry. It began as a dairy farm and evolved into a golf course before becoming a residential community in 1947.

COLUMBUS township (Anoka County) was named in honor of Christopher Columbus.

COLVILLE township (Cook County) honors Col. William Colvill, to whose name a silent *e* was added. A former newspaper publisher in Red Wing, he led the First Minnesota in a famous charge at the battle of Gettysburg.

COMFORT township (Kanabec County) does not necessarily offer succor to citizens or visitors but rather takes its name from a popular late-nineteenth-century magazine, as suggested by its first town clerk, Harry Stone. Lake Comfort (Chisago County) bears the name of county physician John W. Comfort, who likely did offer solace to his patients.

COMFREY city (Brown County) is named for the plant, which the town founder read about in a book.

COMSTOCK city (Clay County) and township (Marshall County) were named in honor of Solomon G. Comstock, a lawyer and prominent nineteenth-century politician.

CONCEPTION village (Wabasha County) was named for the Church of the Immaculate Conception, built here in 1866.

CONEY ISLAND village (Carver County) takes its name from the island in the southern part of Clearwater Lake. The island was named for Coney Island beach of Long Island, N.Y., which Italian immigrants named not for hot dogs, but for its large number of rabbits: *coniglia* in their language, shortened by English speakers to "coney."

CONGER city (Freeborn County) was named by railroad officials for Congressman Edwin H. Conger of Des Moines, Iowa, who was later ambassador to China, Brazil, and Mexico.

COOK COUNTY was named in honor of Maj. Michael Cook, a prominent Faribault citizen and Civil War soldier who was killed at the battle of Nashville. The city (St. Louis County) was named for Wirth H. Cook, a Duluth lumber dealer and later president of the Duluth, Winnipeg and Pacific Railway.

COON CREEK township (Lyon County) has a creek that is a tributary from Dead Coon Lake (Lincoln County), which was named by government surveyors when they found a dead raccoon there.

COON RAPIDS city (Anoka County) was originally called Coon Creek Rapids because of the abundant population of raccoons as well as its location on Coon Creek.

COPAS village (Washington County) was named in honor of John Copas, an Italian immigrant who served in the Fourth Minnesota Regiment during the Civil War.

CORCORAN city and township (Hennepin County) were named for Patrick B. Corcoran, who was the area's first schoolteacher, merchant, and postmaster.

CORINNA township (Wright County) was settled by families from Maine and received its name from Elder Robinson, a Baptist preacher, for his former home.

CORMANT township (Beltrami County) is named, with shortened form, for the Cormorant River, which flows through it and whose name refers to a type of duck. *See* Black Duck

CORNISH township (Aitkin County) is neither noted nor named for game hens, but rather commemorates early settlers Charles and Milo Cornish, while another township (Sibley County) was named by J. B. Wakefield in honor of his native New Hampshire town.

CORVUSO village (Meeker County) is corrupted Latin for "gathering of the crows," named by an early resident for the number of crows present.

COSMOS township (Meeker County) takes its name from an ancient Greek word meaning "order, harmony," proposed by an early settler, perhaps expressing his hopes for his new home.

COTTAGE GROVE city and township (Washington County) were named for the area's mingled groves and prairies.

COTTONWOOD COUNTY and river derive their name from the cottonwood trees along the river. The city and lake (Lyon County) are likewise named for the native trees.

COWHORN lake (Itasca County) is named for its shape.

CRATE township (Chippewa County) was named by citizens in honor of Fanning L. Beasley, an early homesteader. Locating "Crate" in Mr. Beasley's name is something of a trick: it was his nickname, taken from his middle name, Lucretius.

CREDIT RIVER township (Scott County) is named for the stream flowing through it, which appears on Joseph Nicollet's map as "the Credit or Erakah River." The origin of the name is unknown.

CROKE township (Traverse County) was named in honor of Thomas W. Croke, who served as a Catholic bishop in Australia and, later, as an archbishop in Ireland.

CROOKSTON city (Polk County) is the county seat and was named in honor of Col. William Crooks, a Civil War veteran with the Sixth Minnesota Regiment. He served as a state representative and state senator and was chief engineer in bringing the railroad here. The town also honors his father, Ramsay Crooks, president of the American Fur Company.

CROSBY city (Crow Wing County) was named in honor of George H. Crosby, an iron mine manager, while the township (Pine County) was named for pioneer farmer Ira Crosby.

CROW WING COUNTY and township were named for the river, translated from the Ojibwe as "Raven Feather River," for an island in the shape of a crow's wing.

CRYSTAL city and township (Hennepin County) take their name from the lake, which was noted for its deep water and good shores.

CUBA township (Becker County) is named for Cuba, N.Y., the home of an early settler, while the village (Cass County) commemorates the Spanish-American War.

CURRIE city (Murray County) was founded in 1872 by Neil Currie and his father, Archibald Currie, who built a flour mill and engaged in mercantile and banking businesses here.

CUSTER township (Lyon County) was named in 1876 in honor of Gen. George Armstrong Custer, famous for the Battle of Little Big Horn.

CUT FOOT SIOUX lake (Itasca County) is translated from its Ojibwe name, referring to a Dakota man who was maimed and killed here in a 1748 battle.

CUYUNA city and iron ore range (Crow Wing County) were named by Cuyler Adams, a mine owner, who blended his name with that of his dog, Una, who accompanied him on many prospecting trips.

CYPHERS railroad station (Cass County) is not, as the name might suggest, a place of no importance; rather, it is named for a former resident.

DAHLGREN township (Carver County) honors Civil War admiral John A. B. Dahlgren, who invented the Dahlgren gun.

DAKOTA COUNTY and city (Winona County) were named for the Dakota people, the word meaning "alliance" or "league."

DALBO township (Isanti County) has a Swedish name for the home of settlers from the former province of Dalarne, also called Dalecarlia, in central Sweden.

DANEBOD village (Lincoln County) was developed by a colony of Danes and shares its name with Queen Thyra of tenth-century Denmark, meaning "one who mends or saves the Danes."

DARFUR city (Watonwan County) was named either for a region of Sudan or when two Scandinavian railroad men questioned, "why you stop dar fur?"

DARLING township (Morrison County) may well be cherished by its residents, but it takes its name from William L. Darling of St. Paul, who became chief engineer of the Northern Pacific Railroad in 1905.

DARNEN township (Stevens County) had many Irish immigrants who probably proposed the township's original name, Darien, which evolved in spelling to Derrynane and eventually to Darnen. *See also* Derrynane

DASSEL city and township (Meeker County) commemorate Bernard Dassel, who in 1869 was the secretary of the St. Paul and Pacific Railroad Company.

DAVENPORT township (Crow Wing County) honors Col. William Davenport, commandant of Fort Snelling.

DAWSON city (Lac qui Parle County) takes its name from William Dawson, a St. Paul banker who was one of the proprietors of the site.

DAYTON city and township (Hennepin County) honor Lyman Dayton of St. Paul, one of the site's original proprietors.

DEAD LAKE township (Otter Tail County) took the name of its large lake and river; the meaning translated from the Ojibwe refers to a grave or "House of the Dead." In about 1843, thirty or forty Ojibwe old men, women, and children were killed by a war party of Dakota near the lake.

DEBS post office (Beltrami County) honors the socialist activist Eugene V. Debs.

DECORIA township (Blue Earth County) commemorates a Winnebago (Ho-Chunk) leader who, having lost an eye, was called "One-eyed Dekora." A fine orator, he was also known as "Wonderful Decorah" for his wise counsel.

DEEPHAVEN city (Hennepin County) was named by Mrs. Hazen J. Burton, the wife of its first mayor, with the title of a book by Sarah Orne Jewett.

DEERFIELD township (Cass County) was named, as requested by its people, for the plentiful deer here.

DELANO city (Wright County) was named for Francis R. Delano, a St. Croix valley lumberman who later became the first warden of the Minnesota State Prison.

DELAVAN township (Faribault County) was named in honor of Oren Delavan Brown, an engineer on surveys for the Southern Minnesota Railroad.

DELFT village (Cottonwood County) was named for a city in Holland.

DENT city (Otter Tail County) was named for Northwestern Dent Corn, a variety that was grown by farmers throughout the area.

DENTAYBOW township (Koochiching County) honors three of its homestead farmers, named Densmore, Taylor, and Bowman, each represented by a syllable in the name.

DERRYNANE township (Le Sueur County) was partly settled by Irish immigrants, who took this name from Derrynane Abbey, located on the southwest coast of Ireland.

DES MOINES RIVER township (Murray County) is crossed by the river of the same name, which has its sources in the western edge of this county. Originally named for the Indian village Moingona, mispronunciation led to its current name, which is French for "River of the Monks."

DETROIT LAKES city (Becker County) is the county seat and draws its name from the lake, which in turn was named by a French Catholic missionary who camped on the north shore of the lake in full view of the long bar stretching nearly across it and leaving a strait (*detroit* in French) between its two parts.

DEVIL TRACK lake and river (Cook County) were named by Indians. The name implies something supernatural about the lake, translated as "the spirits walking-place-on-the-ice river," but without the supremely evil idea that is suggested by the white settlers' translation to "devil."

DEWEY townships (Itasca and Roseau Counties) commemorate Adm. George Dewey, hero in the Spanish-American War.

DIARRHOEA river (Cook County) receives the outflow of Trout Lake and has this name on maps published from 1851 to 1911, referring to illness thought to come from drinking its water. However, subsequent maps of the Minnesota Geological Survey give it the prosaic title of Greenwood River.

DILWORTH city (Clay County) has a name honoring coffee importer and Pittsburgh resident Joseph Dilworth, who became one of the largest landholders along the Northern Pacific Railroad, of which he was an original stockholder.

DINNER CREEK township (Koochiching County) is crossed by a creek of the same name, where timber cruisers and estimators met for a meal.

DODGE CENTER city (Dodge County) had its name proposed by D. C. Fairbank, for its location at the center of the county.

DODGE COUNTY honors Henry Dodge, governor of Wisconsin, and his son, Augustus C. Dodge, who became an Iowa senator and U.S. minister to Spain.

DOLLYMONT township (Traverse County) bears the name of a seaside suburb of Dublin, Ireland, and may have been named in honor of pioneer settler Anthony Doll.

DONNELLY townships (Marshall and Stevens Counties) commemorate Ignatius Donnelly, noted nineteenth-century Minnesota lawyer, populist politician, and author.

DORAN city (Wilkin County) was named by James J. Hill for his friend Michael Doran, a native of Ireland who was a Le Sueur County banker before moving to St. Paul and serving several terms as a state senator.

DOROTHY village (Red Lake County) was named for St. Dorothy's Catholic Church, which was built in 1880 for the French Canadian families in the area. The name in Greek means "the gift of God."

DOTY railroad station (Olmsted County) was named by G. W. Van Dusen of Rochester, on whose farm this station was located, for James D. Doty, former governor of Wisconsin.

DOUGLAS COUNTY and the township (Dakota County) are named for the Illinois congressman and senator, Stephen A. Douglas, who ran for president against Abraham Lincoln and championed Minnesota's application for statehood.

DOVRE township (Kandiyohi County) received its name from its prominent hills, which early Norwegian settlers called the Dovre Hills in remembrance of Norway's Dovrefjeld Mountains.

DRYDEN township (Sibley County) was named for the celebrated English poet and dramatist John Dryden, upon the request of Hamilton Beatty, the chairman of the township's first board of supervisors.

DULUTH city (St. Louis County) is the county seat, named for the French explorer Daniel Greysolon, sieur Du Luth, who landed on this site in 1679.

DUNDAS city (Rice County) bears the name of a large town in Ontario, and of villages in Ohio, Illinois, and Wisconsin, commemorating Henry Dundas, an eminent eighteenth-century British statesman.

DUNDEE city (Nobles County) has the name of the city in Scotland.

DUNNELL city (Martin County) was named in honor of Mark H. Dunnell, a representative to Congress from 1871 to 1883 and from 1889 to 1891.

DUTCH CHARLEY'S creek (Cottonwood County) was named by government surveyors for the county's first settler, Charles Zierke, who was already living beside the creek when they arrived.

EAGAN township (Dakota County) was named for Patrick Eagan, one of its first settlers.

EAGLE mountain (Cook County) is the highest elevation in Minnesota, 2,301 feet, and a gathering place for eagles.

EAGLE BEND city (Todd County) received this name from its location at a notable bend of Eagle Creek, which was named for the bald eagles found here and throughout the state.

EAGLE LAKE city (Blue Earth County) received its name from the neighboring lake, which U.S. land surveyors had named for the many bald eagles nesting in high trees on the lakeshore.

EAGLE ROCKS and **CHIMNEY ROCK** formations (Fillmore County) rise to an elevation of 1,085 feet and are craggily eroded forms of limestone caused by slow channeling of the valley by the south branch of the Root River.

EAST GRAND FORKS city (Polk County) is on the east side of the Red River, opposite the city of Grand Forks, N.Dak., where the confluence of the Red Lake River with the upper part of the Red River presents two navigable courses, or forks, for travelers.

EASTERN and **WESTERN** townships (Otter Tail County) were named in reference to each other; the former is the most southeastern township in the county, and the latter is the most southwestern township.

ECHOLS village (Watonwan County) was named by officers of the Minneapolis and St. Louis Railroad. This rare geographic name, shared with locations in Georgia and Kentucky, is of unknown origin.

EDDY townships (Clearwater and Roseau Counties) were named in honor of Frank Marion Eddy, a representative to Congress and editor of the *Sauk Centre Herald*.

EDEN township (Brown County) was named because of the settlers' appreciation for the beauty of its scenery and fertility of its soil, while two other townships (Pipestone and Polk Counties) were named for similar reasons by popular vote.

EDEN PRAIRIE city and township (Hennepin County) take their name from author Elizabeth F. Elliot, who used the word "Eden" when expressing her admiration for "this beautiful prairie."

EDEN VALLEY township (Meeker and Stearns County) was named by officers of the Minneapolis, St. Paul and Sault Ste. Marie Railroad. It had previously been known as Pappelbusch, German for the nearby stand of poplar trees.

EDGERTON city (Pipestone County) was named in honor of Gen. Alonzo J. Edgerton, who fought with the Tenth Minnesota Regiment and served as a state senator and, later, as a U.S. senator by appointment.

EDINA city (Hennepin County) took its name from a flour mill owned by Andrew and John Craik, who named their mill in memory of their boyhood home near Edinburgh, Scotland.

EDISON township (Swift County) was named in honor of the inventor Thomas Alva Edison.

EFFIE city (Itasca County) was named for Effie Wenaus, daughter of the first postmaster, Eva Wenaus.

EGLON township (Clay County) bears the name of a city of ancient Palestine. It may have earned its name when an early settler called the area *Ek Land*, Norwegian for "Oakland," because the woodland was mostly oak trees. Pronounced *Egland*, the name was shortened by the locals to Eglon.

ELBA township (Winona County) takes the name of an Italian island famed for its rich ore deposits.

ELBOW LAKE city and township (Grant County) take the name of the adjacent lake that is shaped like an arm bent at the elbow. The city is the county seat.

ELDRED village (Polk County) was named for its founder, John Elg. But Mr. Elg was no Eldred. The name originally was Eldridge, a form of his name, but Minnesota already had an Eldridge, so city fathers settled on Eldred, which may or may not make sense.

ELK RIVER city and township (Sherburne County) are named for the river, home to herds of elk seen by Zebulon Pike and other early explorers and fur traders. The city is the county seat.

ELLENDALE city (Steele County) has a name given in memory of Ellen Dale, who was known for her generosity and kindness to hundreds of railroad employees.

ELLINGTON township (Dodge County) was named for the town in Connecticut.

ELLSWORTH city (Nobles County) was named for Eugene Ellsworth of Cedar Falls, Iowa, for reasons unknown, while the township (Meeker County) was named in honor of Col. Ephraim E. Ellsworth, an early casualty of the Civil War.

ELMORE city and township (Faribault County) were named for Andrew E. Elmore, a prominent citizen of Wisconsin who had many friends among this area's early settlers. The city is the hometown of former U.S. vice president Walter Mondale.

ELY city, lake, and island (St. Louis County) were named in honor of Arthur Ely, one of the financial backers of the construction of the Duluth and Iron Range Railroad.

ELYSIAN city, township, and lake (Le Sueur County) take a name adopted from the Greek *Elysium* and the Elysian Fields, "the dwelling place of the happy souls after death." Presumably this applies equally to the living.

EMBARRASS city and township (St. Louis County) share their name with the river, originally named with a French word referring to the driftwood on parts of this stream, which presumably placed canoeists in compromising positions. *See* Zumbro

EMILY city and township (Crow Wing County) were named for the lake, which likely commemorates a relative of an early lumberman.

ERIN township (Rice County) received this ancient name of Ireland by a vote of citizens, many of them immigrants from the Emerald Isle.

ESKO village (Carlton County) has a Finnish personal name.

ESQUAGAMAH township (Aitkin County) and
ESQUAGAMA lake (St. Louis County) have an Ojibwe
name meaning "the last lake." The township shares its
name with the final and most western in a series of three
nearby lakes.

ETNA village (Fillmore County) was named by drawing
lots when townspeople could not decide among many
choices. It is the name of a famous volcano in Sicily.

EUCLID city and township (Polk County) were named by
Springer Harbaugh, manager of a large farm in Norman
County, for Euclid Avenue in Cleveland, Ohio, his for-
mer home.

EUGENE township (Lake of the Woods County) was
probably named for Eugene V. Debs, three-time presidential candidate of the Socialist Party.

EUREKA township (Dakota County) has for its name the
Greek expression, "I have found it," which was the exclamation of settlers upon their arrival in 1854.

EVANSVILLE township (Douglas County) commemorates
its first mail carrier, Albert Evans.

EVELETH city (St. Louis County) is located on the Mesabi
Range and was named for Erwin Eveleth, former postmaster and mayor of Corunna, Mich. While traveling as
a timber cruiser in the area, Eveleth found that his com-
pass suggested the presence of iron.

EVERGLADE township (Stevens County) for unknown
reasons is named for the Florida Everglades, despite the
absence of alligators and other inhabitants of that
southern marshland.

EXCEL township (Marshall County) was named for the city of Excelsior (Hennepin County), with a shortened form to avoid repetition.

EXCELSIOR city and township (Hennepin County) were founded by a group of colonists, the Excelsior Pioneer Association, taking the name from Henry W. Longfellow's poem, "Excelsior."

EYOTA city and township (Olmsted County) are named with this Dakota word meaning "greatest, most," possibly because settlers envisioned grandeur for these places.

FAHLUN township (Kandiyohi County) and **FALUN** township (Roseau County) bear the name of an important mining town in central Sweden, sometimes called "the Treasury of Sweden" for its copper, silver, and gold mines.

FAIR HAVEN township (Stearns County) received its name from an exclamation of Thomas C. Partridge, who upon his arrival said, "This is a fair haven!"

FAIRFAX city (Renville County) was named by Eben Ryder, president of the Minneapolis and St. Louis Railroad Company, for his native county in Virginia.

FAIRMONT city (Martin County) is the county seat and was first called Fair Mount, referring to its view overlooking the Central Chain of lakes.

FALCON HEIGHTS city (Ramsey County) was named by a real estate investor named Faulkner, for what reason we do not know.

FALL LAKE township (Lake County) is named for the lake, which was known by the Ojibwe as *Kawasachong*, meaning "mist or foam lake," referring to the mist and spray rising from the rapids and falls of the Kawishiwi River.

FARIBAULT COUNTY and city (Rice County) honor a father and son: the county was named for Jean Baptiste Faribault, a long-time trader among the Dakota, while the city, which is the county seat, commemorates his son, Alexander, who established trading routes in this and other Minnesota counties.

FARM ISLAND township (Aitkin County) shares its name with a lake that has a twenty-nine-acre island on which the Ojibwe cultivated crops.

FARMINGTON townships (Dakota and Olmsted Counties) received their names from their locations, which proved to be excellent areas for farming.

FARWELL city (Pope County) possibly takes its name from a form of the Norwegian word *farväl,* meaning "farewell."

FELTON city and township (Clay County) were named for Samuel M. Felton by Great Northern Railway officers, or for William Felton, a representative in the state legislature.

FERGUS FALLS city and township (Otter Tail County) are named for James Fergus, a resident of Little Falls who, although he financed the expedition that founded the city, never actually visited the site. The city is the county seat.

FERTILE city (Polk County) was named for the village in Worth County in northern Iowa, where some of its first settlers formerly resided.

FILLMORE COUNTY and township were named for President Millard Fillmore. He held the office during negotiations concerning Minnesota's statehood.

FINLAND village (Lake County) was developed primarily by Finnish immigrants and is named in honor of them.

FISHER city and township (Polk County) first had the name Shirt-tail Bend because a shirt had been tied to a pole to warn steamboats of the bend in the Red Lake River. The city and township honor William H. Fisher, a railroad executive for various companies.

FLOODWOOD city and township (St. Louis County) are located at the mouth of the Floodwood River, which was often obstructed by rafts of driftwood.

FLORA township (Renville County) does not honor a local woman of prominence but instead commemorates a horse: the first one brought here by Francis Shoemaker.

FLORIAN village (Marshall County) was named by early Polish settlers for Father Florian Matuszewske, who opened a post office here in 1903.

FLORIDA lake (Kandiyohi County) was possibly named by early settlers because of its location to the south of the nearby Norway Lake. The township (Yellow Medicine County) is named for its lake, which honors a railway contractor who had a camp here.

FLOUR lake (Cook County) received its name because a cache of flour was placed here during government surveys.

FLOWING township (Clay County) was settled by Scandinavians who adopted this name. The name may refer to the numerous artesian or flowing wells.

FOGG lake (Mille Lacs County) has a name that refers not to atmospheric conditions but instead to settler Frederick A. Fogg.

FOLEY city (Benton County) was named for its founder, John Foley, who led the successful drive to move the county seat from Sauk Rapids to Foley.

FOND DU LAC site (St. Louis County) bears a French name that signifies "farther end of the lake," or, more commonly, "head of the lake."

FOOT lake (Kandiyohi County) is not named for its shape or location, but rather commemorates Solomon R. Foot, the first settler of Willmar Township.

FORADA city (Douglas County) uses the first name of Mrs. Cyrus A. Campbell, whose husband first platted the section. Her name was Ada, but that name was already registered as the seat of Norman County, so the prefix was added.

FORD township (Kanabec County) was named for Henry Ford, the automobile manufacturer who was campaigning for world peace in 1915, when the township was organized.

FOREST LAKE city and township (Washington County) took the name of the lake, which describes the heavy timber along its shores.

FORT RIPLEY city and township (Crow Wing County) share their name with the former fort (Morrison County), now the Camp Ripley Military Reservation, which was named in honor of Gen. Eleazar W. Ripley, who served in the War of 1812.

FOSSTON city (Polk County) was named for early merchant Louis Foss, who later moved to Washington State.

FOSTER township (Faribault County) was named for Dr. Reuben R. Foster, one of the county's first resident physicians.

FOUNTAIN township (Fillmore County) was named for its large natural spring.

FOUR-LEGGED lake and creek (Clearwater County) are named with a translation from the Ojibwe for an old Indian who lived here.

FRANCONIA township (Chisago County) was named by the first settler, Ansel Smith, for his hometown in the White Mountains of New Hampshire or to honor his son, Francis, who died in infancy.

FRANKLIN city (Renville County) and townships (Itasca and Wright Counties) were named in honor of Benjamin Franklin, American philosopher, statesman, diplomat, and author.

FRAZEE city (Becker County) was named in honor of Randolph L. Frazee, owner of its lumber mill, flour mill, and general store.

FREEBORN COUNTY and township were named in honor of William Freeborn, council member in the territorial legislature from 1854 to 1857.

FREEDHEM village (Morrison County) was settled by Swedes, who named the community Fridhem, a common Swedish place name meaning "home of peace," the spelling of which was later altered to Freedhem.

FREEDOM township (Waseca County) was named by homestead farmer Fletcher D. Seaman and shares its name with locations in ten other states.

FREELAND township (Lac qui Parle County) is named for J. P. Free, one of its pioneers. Petitioners first requested the name Freedom, but another township had already claimed that name.

FREEPORT city (Stearns County) was named by settlers from Freeport, Ill.

FRENCH LAKE township (Wright County) is named for its largest lake and a creek, which honor French Canadian settlers.

FRIDLEY township (Anoka County) commemorates Abram M. Fridley, an agent for the Winnebago (Ho-Chunk) Indians who later became a farmer and state legislator.

FRONTENAC village (Goodhue County) commemorates Louis de Buade de Frontenac, a French colonial governor of Canada, though there is no record of his setting foot in the area.

FROST city (Faribault County) isn't any colder than other settlements. Its name honors a nineteenth-century Chicago architect, Charles S. Frost.

FULDA city (Murray County) was named for an ancient city in central Germany on the river Fulda, noted for its early medieval abbey and cathedral.

FUNKLEY city (Beltrami County) was named for Henry Funkley, a county attorney at the turn of the twentieth century.

GARDEN CITY township (Blue Earth County) was named in reference to the native floral charms of the area, "like a garden of wild flowers."

GARFIELD city (Douglas County) and townships (Lac qui Parle and Polk Counties) were named in honor of President James A. Garfield, who was shot on July 2, 1881, and died September 19, 1881.

GARNES township (Red Lake County) takes the name of E. K. Garnes, an early settler from Norway. It may also be a phonetic spelling of the first postmaster's surname: Gjernes.

GARY city (Norman County) was named in honor of Garrett L. Thorpe, its first merchant.

GAYLORD city (Sibley County) is the county seat and commemorates Edward W. Gaylord, an executive of the Minneapolis and St. Louis Railroad Company.

GENNESSEE township (Kandiyohi County) was named, with changed spelling, for the Genesee River in New York, where several of its pioneers had previously lived. This Indian name means "shining valley" or "beautiful valley."

GENTILLY township (Polk County) took its name from a village on the St. Lawrence River in Quebec, which was named for the southern suburb of Paris, France. Settled by Catholics, the village was originally a rest stop for the stage line.

GEORGETOWN city (Clay County) honors Sir George Simpson, governor of the Hudson's Bay Company, which established a trading post here in 1859.

GHENT city (Lyon County) was named for the ancient Belgian city by colonists from Belgium, perhaps also in reference to Robert Browning's poem "How They Brought the Good News from Ghent to Aix."

GIBBON city (Sibley County) is named for Gen. John Gibbon, a commandant at Fort Snelling from 1880 to 1882, or for Edward Gibbon, an English historian.

GILBERT city (St. Louis County) was named in honor of E. A. Gilbert, a prominent Duluth businessman, or for Giles Gilbert, who owned nearby mining and timber land.

GILCHRIST township (Pope County) was named by combining the first syllables of the surnames of early settlers Ole Gilbertson and Gunder Christopherson.

GLENCOE city and township (McLeod County) were named by Martin McLeod in commemoration of the valley of Glencoe in Scotland. The city is the county seat.

GLENDORADO township (Benton County) received its name, which is partly Spanish, meaning "the golden glen," by petition of its settlers.

GLENWOOD city and township (Pope County) are situated at the northeast end of Lake Minnewaska and were named for the great glen or valley occupied by the lake and for the woods around its shores, which contrast with the surrounding prairie. The city is the county seat.

GLORY post office (Aitkin County) takes its name from the refrain of the "Battle Hymn of the Republic": "Glory, Glory, Hallelujah."

GLUEK village (Chippewa County) takes its name from the Gluek Brewing Company, which financed the completion of a rail line serving the community.

GLYNDON city and township (Clay County) are named for a popular writer of *Atlantic Hearth and Home,* Laura Catherine Redden Searing, who used the *nom de plume* Howard Glyndon.

GODAHL village (Watonwan County) was named by early Norwegian settlers from Gode Dahl, which means "good valley."

GOLDEN VALLEY city (Hennepin County) is named for its beautiful valley enclosing a small and narrow lake.

GONVICK city (Clearwater County) may have been named for two different people. One version is that a group of residents decided to name it for the oldest man present, Martin Gonvick, born in 1863. The other story is that it was named for Emma Gonvick Monsrud, wife of area sawmill owner Peter Monsrud.

GOOD HOPE townships (Itasca and Norman Counties) received their auspicious names by vote of their residents.

GOOD THUNDER city (Blue Earth County) was named for a leader of the Winnebago (Ho-Chunk) whose village was near this site, or for a Dakota named *Wa-kin-yan-was-te*, translated as "Good Thunder." Both men were friendly to white settlers.

GOODHUE COUNTY and township were named in honor of James M. Goodhue, the first printer and editor in Minnesota, who published the first issue of the *Minnesota Pioneer* on April 28, 1849.

GOODRIDGE city and township (Pennington County) are named for a broad but very low ridge that extends from the original village about four miles southeastward.

GOODVIEW city (Winona County) is located in the Mississippi River valley, and its residents likely chose a name that described their surroundings.

GOOSEBERRY river (Lake County) may be named with a translation from the Ojibwe or, as others have suggested, with the anglicization of Groseilliers, for the French explorer Médard Chouart, sieur des Groseilliers.

GÖTAHOLM village (Carver County) combines Göta, for Götaland, Sweden, where most early settlers came from, and Holm, an abbreviation of the Latin *Holmiensis,* for Stockholm.

GRACEVILLE township (Big Stone County) was founded by Catholic colonists and named in honor of Thomas L. Grace, a bishop of St. Paul. Another history of this place name is that it is for Grace McDonald, the first white child born here.

GRAHAM LAKES township (Nobles County) received this name from its East and West Graham Lakes, named for James D. Graham, a commissioner for the international boundary survey.

GRANADA city (Martin County) bears the name of the medieval Moorish city and kingdom in Spain.

GRAND LAKE township and river (St. Louis County) are named for the nearby lake, which is much larger than a number of neighboring lakes.

GRAND MARAIS city and township (Cook County) were given this French name, meaning "great marsh," by fur traders. The city is the county seat.

GRAND MEADOW city and township (Mower County) were named by county commissioners because of their extensive prairie.

GRAND PORTAGE village (Cook County) has the distinction of being the most eastern and oldest settlement of white men in the area of Minnesota. It marked the portage from Lake Superior to the Pigeon River.

GRAND RAPIDS city and township (Itasca County) are named for their location beside rapids of the Mississippi River. The city is the county seat.

GRANGE township (Pipestone County) was named in honor of the Patrons of Husbandry, an agricultural order whose lodges are called granges, from the French words for "barn" and "farmer." The order was founded in 1867 by a Minnesotan, Oliver H. Kelley, who farmed in Sherburne County.

GRANITE FALLS city (Chippewa and Yellow Medicine Counties) and township (Chippewa County) were named for the granite and gneiss outcrops of the Minnesota River here, which contribute to a fall of thirty-eight feet. The city is the Yellow Medicine county seat.

GRANT COUNTY and city (Washington County) were named in honor of Ulysses S. Grant, Civil War commander of Union troops and later president of the United States.

GRAPELAND post office (Faribault County) was named for wild grapes growing along the Maple River.

GREAT SCOTT township (St. Louis County) was named by the board of county commissioners for a common exclamation of one of the board members.

GREEN LAKE township (Kandiyohi County) is named for the nearby lake, noted by early settlers for its bottle-green shade.

GREENBUSH city (Roseau County) was named for the evergreen trees seen near the "ridge road" as settlers approached eastward from the Red River Valley, while the township (Mille Lacs County) was named by early lumbermen and farmers for a place in Maine, their former home.

GREENFIELD city (Hennepin County) was incorporated in 1958 and took its name in part from Greenwood Township, a village platted a century earlier by Thomas A. Holmes that was superseded by Rockford. Greenwood was named for its "charming woodlands," seen by its first settlers in the early days of summer.

GREENWAY township (Itasca County) was named for John C. Greenway, who formerly operated the Oliver Mining Company in Coleraine on the Mesabi Range.

GREY CLOUD ISLAND township (Washington County) was named for the island and the noted Dakota woman who lived there.

GREY EAGLE township (Todd County) was named for an eagle shot here in 1868 by A. M. Crowell, who later became a municipal judge in Bemidji.

GRINDSTONE river and lake (Pine County) are named for the gritty sandstone outcrop on the north side of the river, used by Indians and early fur traders for sharpening iron and steel tools.

GRIT post office (Red Lake County) supposedly had its name chosen because it required considerable "grit" to haul goods on the twenty miles of bad road from Lambert.

GROUNDHOUSE village and river (Kanabec County) were named for wooden earth-covered huts, homes to the Hidatsa Indians who once lived in the area.

GROW township (Anoka County) was named to honor Galusha A. Grow, a Pennsylvania congressman who introduced a free homestead bill in the legislature for ten years until it was adopted in 1862. His perseverance endeared him to millions of American homesteaders.

GRYGLA city (Marshall County) was named for the "Father of the Polish National Alliance," Frank Grygla.

GUCKEEN village (Faribault County) was named for Patrick Guckeen, on whose land the town site was located.

GULL lake and river and East Gull Lake township (Cass County) were named with a translation from their Ojibwe name, which meant "the-place-of-young-gulls."

HACKENSACK city (Cass County) derived its name from Hackensack, N.J., but it is unclear where the name originated. Hackensack is also known as the home of Paul Bunyan's girlfriend, Lucette Diana Kensack.

HALE township (McLeod County) was named either for an early settler or for John P. Hale, a senator from New Hampshire and the Free Soil Party presidential candidate in 1852.

HALFWAY brook (Benton County) is a tributary to the Mississippi River north of Sartell and received this name because it is nearly midway between Sauk Rapids and Watab.

HALLOCK city and township (Kittson County) were named in honor of one of the village founders, Charles Hallock, a widely known sportsman, journalist, and author and the founder and editor of *Forest and Stream* magazine. The city is the county seat.

HAM LAKE city and township (Anoka County) are named for the lake, which was named for its shape.

HAMBURG city (Carver County) was named for the German port city.

HANCOCK city (Stevens County) is named for Joseph Woods Hancock, who came to Minnesota as a missionary teacher, then served as a pastor and superintendent of schools for Goodhue County.

HANSKA city and township (Brown County) are named for the nearby body of water, a narrow lake referred to by the Dakota with their word for "long" or "tall."

HAPPYLAND railroad station (Koochiching County) has several stories regarding the origin of its name. The most prominent recounts that in 1907 railroad construction crews had mosquitoes and a muskeg bog to contend with, but when they reached a high pine area south of Littlefork the mosquitoes let up and walking was easier, so the crew named it a "happy land."

HARMONY city and township (Fillmore County) are named in accord with places in fifteen other states.

HARRIET lake (Hennepin County) was named for Harriet Leavenworth, wife of Col. Harry Leavenworth, first commandant at Fort Snelling.

HARRIS township (Itasca County) was named for Duncan Harris, who owned a fruit farm here.

HARTLAND city and township (Freeborn County) take their name from Hartland in Windsor County, Vt., the former home of early settlers.

HASSAN township (Hennepin County) received its name from the Dakota word *chanhassen*, meaning "the sugar maple tree": *chan*, tree, and *hassen,* from *haza,* the huckleberry or blueberry; that is, the tree having similarly sweet sap.

HASSEL lake (Swift County) has a Norwegian name meaning "hazel."

HASTINGS city (Dakota County) is the county seat and was named when several town proprietors drew lots.

The middle name of Henry Hastings Sibley, later governor and general, was the winner.

HASTY village (Wright County) refers neither to pudding nor to speed, but rather commemorates Warren Hasty, on whose farm the village was platted in 1895.

HATFIELD city (Pipestone County) may have been named, according to a local story, because a member of a railroad grading crew had trouble keeping his hat on during a period of strong winds. After retrieving it from the field a number of times, he suggested the name "hat field."

HAVANA township (Steele County) took this name at Elijah Easton's request, for the county seat of Mason County, Ill. A Spanish word meaning "a haven, a harbor," Havana later became the name of Cuba's capital as well.

HAVELOCK township (Chippewa County) was named in honor of the English general Sir Henry Havelock, hero of the siege of Lucknow, India, in 1857.

HAVEN township (Sherburne County) may offer refuge for some, but it is named for John O. Haven, who held numerous county offices including registrar of deeds and superintendent of schools.

HAWLEY city and township (Clay County) were named in honor of Gen. Joseph R. Hawley, an original stockholder in the Northern Pacific Railroad who served in the Union Army during the Civil War and was later a U.S. senator.

HAYFIELD city and township (Dodge County) adopted their name from a township of Crawford County in northwestern Pennsylvania.

HAZEL village (Pennington County) is named for the two species of hazel nuts common in this area.

HAZEL RUN city and township (Yellow Medicine County) bear the name of the creek, a tributary to the Minnesota River that was bordered by hazel bushes.

HECTOR city and township (Renville County) were named by settlers for their previous home in Schuyler County, N.Y.

HEIGHT OF LAND township (Becker County) is named for the large lake crossed by its north boundary. It is translated from the Ojibwe, meaning "the lake where the portage is across a divide separating water which runs different ways."

HENDERSON city and township (Sibley County) were named by Joseph R. Brown, who is commemorated by Brown County, in honor of his father's sister, Margaret Brown Henderson, and her son, Andrew Henderson.

HENDRUM city and township (Norman County) are named for a district or group of farms in Norway, the former home of early settlers.

HENNEPIN COUNTY and lake and river commemorate the Franciscan missionary Louis Hennepin, who explored the upper Mississippi River from 1678 to 1680.

HENNING city and township (Otter Tail County) honor John O. Henning, the town's druggist.

HEREFORD village (Grant County) residents wanted to name the place Culbertson, in honor of a man who owned a tract of land here, but Mr. Culbertson said if they wished to compliment him, they should name it

Hereford for his beautiful herd of white-faced cattle. This breed was named for a county in England.

HERMAN city (Grant County) received its name in honor of Herman Trott, land agent of the St. Paul and Pacific Railroad, while the township (St. Louis County) was named by German settlers for their country's early hero, who defended Germany against Roman troops. The township later became Hermantown.

HERON LAKE city and township (Jackson County) were named for the large lake on their west side, which is translated from the Dakota word meaning "the nesting place of herons."

HIBBING city (St. Louis County) was named for its founder, Frank Hibbing, who discovered ore beds here in 1892.

HICKORY township (Pennington County) was named for its location near the northwestern limit of the swamp hickory tree.

HILL township (Kittson County) honors railway magnate James J. Hill, who owned 15,000 acres of farmland in the area.

HILLMAN township (Morrison County) takes its name from the brook, which commemorates a pioneer settler.

HILLS city (Rock County) may seem oddly named, because it and most of this county occupy flat prairie land. The name refers to Frederick C. Hills, who was president of the Sioux City and Northern Railway in 1890.

HINCKLEY city and township (Pine County) were named in honor of Isaac Hinckley, president of the Philadelphia,

Wilmington and Baltimore Railroad Company. He was a stockholder for the construction of the St. Paul and Duluth Railroad.

HODGES township (Stevens County) was named in honor of Leonard B. Hodges, tree planter for the St. Paul, Minneapolis and Manitoba Railroad (later the Great Northern Railway), who set out trees in many villages along this railway.

HOKAH city and township (Houston County) bear the Dakota name for the Root River, which is its English translation.

HOLDINGFORD city and **HOLDING** township (Stearns County) are named in honor of the first permanent settler, Randolph Holding, who arrived in 1868.

HOLLANDALE city (Freeborn County) is named for its many early farm families of Dutch descent.

HOLLY city and township (Murray County) were named for a man who didn't much like it here. John Z. Holly, an early pioneer, returned to his native Illinois after only a few years in his namesake township.

HOLY CROSS township (Clay County) was named for the conspicuous wooden cross set by Father Geniun at a cemetery about a half-mile west of the Red River, in North Dakota. This Minnesota community was comprised of Lutherans who considered themselves part of the "Holy Cross neighborhood."

HOME township (Brown County) was named during a meeting of three township supervisors. The hour grew late, and one impatiently said, "Let's go home," to which another answered, "Let's call it Home Township!"

HOME LAKE township (Norman County) has two small lakes to which this name was given in honor of John Homelvig, the township's former clerk.

HOOK lake (McLeod County) is not hook-shaped but takes its name from Isaac Hook, a recluse who lived here for many years.

HOPKINS city (Hennepin County) commemorates Harley Hopkins, an adventurer and gold prospector who became its first postmaster.

HORSESHOE lake (Aitkin County) is named for its curved shape, as are numerous lakes throughout the state.

HOUSTON COUNTY and township were named for Samuel Houston, the president of Texas before its annexation by the United States and afterward a senator and governor of that state.

HOVLAND township (Cook County) was named by Anna Brunes, for her grandfather's estate in Norway.

HOWARD LAKE city (Wright County) takes its name from the lake of the same designation, which was named for John Howard, an English philanthropist.

HOYT LAKES city and township (St. Louis County) were named by their developer, Pickands Mather and Company, for its director, Elton Hoyt II.

HUBBARD COUNTY and township (Polk County) were named in honor of Lucius F. Hubbard, a general in the Civil War and governor of Minnesota.

HUGO city (Washington County) was named in honor of Trevanion William Hugo, chief engineer of the Consolidated Elevator Company and mayor of Duluth from 1900 to 1904.

HUNGRY JACK lake (Cook County) refers to a government surveyor, Andrew Jackson Scott, who while at this lake was forced to diet due to scanty food supplies.

HURRICANE lake (Cottonwood County) more appropriately should have been called Tornado lake, after the storm that uprooted many trees along its shores. As everyone knows, hurricanes don't visit Minnesota.

HUTCHINSON city and township (McLeod County) were founded by the Hutchinson brothers, Asa, Judson, and John, members of the famous family of singers who gave concerts of popular and patriotic songs from 1841 until the close of the Civil War.

HYDE PARK township (Wabasha County) received its name in 1862 at the suggestion of an Englishman, for one of the most famous places in London, England. But the choice of name may also offer tribute to John E. Hyde, a merchant of Mazeppa.

IBERIA village (Brown County) bears the ancient name of the Spanish and Portuguese peninsula.

ICE CRACKING lake (Becker County) is named in translation from the Ojibwe, presumably for the sounds it makes during the winter months.

IDUN township (Aitkin County) was named for a Scandinavian deity's daughter, whose name refers to youth and beauty.

IMOGENE village and lake (Martin County) have the name of a character from a play by William Shakespeare.

INDEPENDENCE city and township (Hennepin County) bear the name of their largest lake, which was christened by a member of a Fourth of July excursionist party, Kelsey Hinman, in honor of the national holiday. Another lake (Jackson County) was named by U.S. surveyors who reached it on the Fourth of July.

INTERNATIONAL FALLS city (Koochiching County) is the county seat and its name reflects its location on the international boundary with Canada at the Koochiching Falls of the Rainy River.

INVER GROVE HEIGHTS city (Dakota County) was named for Inver Grove in Ireland, the previous home of many of its settlers.

IOSCO township (Waseca County) has a name of Algonquin derivation, meaning "water of light" or "shining water."

IRENE lake (Douglas County) honors Irene Roadruck, for whose mother Lake Miltona was named. *See* Miltona

IRVING township (Kandiyohi County) was likely named in honor of the distinguished American author Washington Irving.

ISABELLA village (Lake County) is the "highest" community in the state, 200 feet above sea level. The origin of its name and that of the nearby river and lake is unknown.

ISANTI COUNTY and city and township bear the former name of a large division of the Dakota, anciently Izatys, now Santee, who lived years ago in the region of the Rum River and Mille Lacs. The translation is found in the name of Knife Lake: *isan*, knife, and *ati*, dwell on or at. *See also* Kathio

ITASCA COUNTY derived its name from the lake (Clearwater County), which is the source of the Mississippi River and was named by Henry Schoolcraft. The name was created by writing together two Latin words— *veritas*, truth, and *caput*, head—and cutting off the first and last syllables. A state park (Clearwater County) also carries this name.

IVANHOE city (Lincoln County) was named by railroad officials for the hero of the novel by Sir Walter Scott. Many of the town's street names are for characters in the novel. The city is the county seat.

J

JACKSON township (Scott County) was probably named for President Andrew Jackson.

JACKSON COUNTY and city, the county seat, honor Henry Jackson, St. Paul's first merchant, justice of the peace, and postmaster, though some think it commemorates President Andrew Jackson.

JANESVILLE township (Waseca County) was named by its platter, J. W. Hosmer, for Jane Sprague, presumably an early resident.

JASPER city (Pipestone and Rock Counties) was named for its quarries of red quartzite, commonly called jasper, an excellent building and paving stone.

JESSENLAND city and township (Sibley County) are supposedly named because Jesse Cameron was the first settler here, leading the region to be known as "Jesse's Land."

JO DAVIESS township (Faribault County) commemorates Joseph H. Daviess (pronounced *Davis*), a soldier, lawyer, and orator from Kentucky who was killed in the battle of Tippecanoe, November 7, 1811.

JOHNSONVILLE township (Redwood County) was named for the numerous Johnsons living here when it was organized in 1879. Four officers of the first township board had this surname.

JORDAN city (Scott County) and the township and creeks (Fillmore County) were named for the River Jordan in Palestine.

JUDGE village (Olmsted County) compliments the Judge family, who were among its founders in 1891.

JUDSON township (Blue Earth County) was named in honor of a nineteenth-century Baptist missionary to Burma, Adoniram Judson.

KABEKONA lake and river (Hubbard County) have an Ojibwe name translated by Henry Schoolcraft as "the rest in the path," later defined as "the end of all roads."

KABETOGAMA lake and township (St. Louis County) bear an Ojibwe name meaning "the lake that lies parallel," in this case in relation to Rainy Lake.

KALEVALA township (Carlton County) had many Finnish settlers who chose the name of Finland's national epic poem, meaning "the abode or land of heroes."

KANABEC COUNTY and township use the Ojibwe word for snake, from the Snake River, which flows through Kanabec and Pine Counties.

KANDIYOHI COUNTY and township bear the Dakota name of their lakes, meaning "where the buffalo fish come."

KANDOTA township (Todd County) has a name derived from the Dakota, meaning "Here we rest."

KANSAS lake (Watonwan County) has nothing to do with the state of Kansas, but, in a somewhat distorted form, commemorates John Kensie, an early settler by the lake.

KARLSTAD city (Kittson County) was named for the Swedish city.

KASOTA township (Le Sueur County) took a Dakota name that means "clear or cleared off" and was applied to the nearby bare ridge or prairie plateau of limestone, which is known as kasota stone.

KASSON city (Dodge County) was named in honor of Jabez H. Kasson, owner of the original town site.

KATHIO township (Mille Lacs County) bears an erroneously transcribed form of the name of a Dakota village, Izatys. An early report showed the *Iz* of Izatys as "K" and the *ys* as "hio," and those who followed repeated this error. Thus, while the intended name was Indian in origin, Kathio is merely a mistake.

KAWISHIWI river (Lake County) has an Ojibwe name meaning "the river full of beavers' [or muskrats'] houses."

KEEWATIN city (Itasca County) has an Ojibwe name meaning "north" or the "north wind." The word appears, with a different spelling, in Henry W. Longfellow's *The Song of Hiawatha*.

KELSO township (Sibley County) was named by A. P. Walker for a town in Scotland on the Tweed River.

KEMI post office (Cottonwood County) was given this name by the U.S. Post Office because it was short and different. This assessment remains true today.

KENNETH city (Rock County) was named for the son of early farmer Jay A. Kennicott.

KENSINGTON city (Douglas County) has the name of a western section of London, England, but in Minnesota it is known as the home of the famous Kensington rune stone.

KENYON city and township (Goodhue County) were named for a pioneer merchant who built the first store here in 1855, or for Kenyon College in Gambier, Ohio, the alma mater of one of the town founders.

KERKHOVEN city and township (Swift County) are named in honor of Johannes Kerkhoven, who with his brother, Theodores, was given the contract to build rail lines west from St. Paul to Willmar to Kerkhoven.

KETTLE RIVER city (Carlton County) and township (Pine County) take their name from the river, which was named in reference to rocks eroded by water into kettle shapes.

KEY WEST village (Polk County) probably does not commemorate Florida's vacationland. Its name more likely refers to its location in Keystone Township.

KEYSTONE township (Polk County) had the very large Keystone farm, owned by investors in Pittsburgh, Pa. The farm was named for Pennsylvania's sobriquet, the "Keystone State," which reflects its location at the center of the thirteen original American states, similar to the keystone of an arch.

KIESTER city and township (Faribault County) do not take their name from the common slang term, but rather from Jacob A. Kiester, who became the county's historian.

KILKENNY township (Le Sueur County) was named by its Irish settlers for a city and county of southeastern Ireland.

KINBRAE city (Nobles County) was founded in 1879 by the Dundee Land Company of Scotland, which probably gave the city and adjoining lake their Scottish name.

KING township (Polk County) was named for its first postmaster, Ephraim King. *See also* Queen

KITTSON COUNTY was named in honor of Norman W. Kittson, one of the leading pioneers of the territory and state. He was a fur trader and manager for the American Fur Company, member of the territorial legislature, and owner of the Red River Transportation Company.

KLONDIKE township (Crow Wing County) was named for the gold region in the Yukon district of Canada because of the iron ore deposits here. *Klondike* (or *Throndiuk*) is an Indian word for "river full of fish." In 1918 the town's name was changed to Ironton.

KNATVOLD village (Freeborn County) was named for state senator Thorvald V. Knatvold of Albert Lea.

KNIFE LAKE township (Kanabec County) received its name from the lake and river, which are named with translations from the Dakota and Ojibwe. In the winter of 1659–60, the first knives of iron or steel were obtained by the Dakota, brought here by explorers and the Huron and Ottawa Indians.

KNIFE RIVER village (Lake County) is at the mouth of the river of this name, which is translated from the Ojibwe for an adjoining rock formation, a blue-black siliceous rock with sharp edges.

KOOCHICHING COUNTY bears the Cree name used by the Ojibwe for Rainy Lake as well as the Rainy River and its great falls and rapids at International Falls. The name probably refers to the mist created by the falls. *See* Rainy

KRAGNES village (Clay County) was named in honor of Andrew O. Kragnes, a prominent Norwegian farmer who was one of the area's first settlers.

LAC QUI PARLE COUNTY and township, lake, and river take a French name meaning "the lake that talks," which is translated from the Dakota name, probably suggested by the echoes thrown back from the surrounding bluffs or by the creaks and groans emitted by shifting ice in winter and spring.

LA CRESCENT township (Houston County) was named in allusion to the town of La Crosse, Wis. *La crosse* was the French name for the bat used in playing ball and was applied to the game often played by the Indians. However, the founders of La Crescent confused the name with *la croix,* the cross, and hearkened to the ancient Crusades, where the cross and the crescent were raised in battle. The citizens resolved to challenge their La Crosse rival by naming their town La Crescent.

LA CROIX lake (St. Louis County) was named by French explorers for its cross-like shape.

LA CROSSE township (Jackson County) was named for La Crosse, Wis., an earlier home of many of its first settlers. *La crosse* is the French name for an Indian ball game.

LAFAYETTE city and township (Nicollet County) were named in honor of the Marquis de Lafayette of France, who greatly aided George Washington during the Revolutionary War.

LA GRAND township (Douglas County) was originally called West Alexandria for its location but eventually took its current name, for an early resident of Alexandria.

LAIRD railroad station (Olmsted County) was named in honor of William H. Laird of Winona, a lumber executive, donor of the Winona public library building, and president of the trustees of Carleton College.

LAKE township (Roseau County) is the largest in the county and surrounds the city of Warroad, bordered by Lake of the Woods.

LAKE ALICE township (Hubbard County) is named for the lake, which commemorates Alice Glazier, who accompanied her father, Willard Glazier, on his exploration for the source of the Mississippi River.

LAKE BELT township (Martin County) was named for its series of three lakes. An alternate story is that it was named for Lake Belle (later changed to Clear Lake), but its name was recorded in error.

LAKE BENTON city and township (Lincoln County) bear the name of the lake, which was named by John C. Frémont for Sen. Thomas H. Benton, whose daughter, Jessie, Frémont later married.

LAKE BRONSON city (Kittson County) takes its name from the Giles Bronson family, the first settlers in the area.

LAKE CITY city (Wabasha and Goodhue Counties) was named by its residents, probably in recognition of its location on Lake Pepin.

LAKE COUNTY received its name because it is bounded on the southeast by Lake Superior.

LAKE CRYSTAL city (Blue Earth County) shares its name with the nearby lake, which explorers John Frémont and Joseph Nicollet named for the remarkable purity of its waters.

LAKE ELMO city (Washington County) was named for the adjoining lake, which commemorates the novel *St. Elmo* by Augusta J. Evans. A more recent publication, *Moon Over Lake Elmo* by Steve Thayer, also memorializes the lake.

LAKE FREMONT township (Martin County) was named in honor of John C. Frémont, who, prior to being an army officer and presidential candidate, was an explorer known as "The Pathfinder."

LAKE HUBERT village (Crow Wing County) honors St. Hubert, the patron saint of hunters.

LAKE IDA township (Norman County) bears the name of its small lake, which honors Ida Paulson, daughter of an early homesteader.

LAKE LILLIAN city and township (Kandiyohi County) are named for the lake, which honors the wife of artist and author Edwin Whitefield, who accompanied the first exploring party to the Kandiyohi Lakes in the summer of 1856.

LAKE MARION village (Dakota County) was named in honor of Marion W. Savage, owner of the famous trotting horse, Dan Patch. *See also* Savage

LAKE MARY township (Douglas County) was named for its large lake, which commemorates Mary A. Kinkead, a homesteader in 1861, sister of Alexander Kinkead, for whom Alexandria is named.

LAKE OF THE WOODS COUNTY takes its name from the large lake on the Minnesota-Ontario border (also Roseau County), which French explorers named *Lac des Bois*, from which the English name is translated.

LAKE WOBEGON region (Mist County, thought to be near Stearns County) is popularly known as the state-of-mind hometown of author Garrison Keillor, host of public radio's *A Prairie Home Companion*.

LAKETOWN township (Carver County) was named by John Salter for its ten small lakes and the larger Clearwater Lake to its west.

LAKEVILLE city (Dakota County) received its name from the township, which in turn was named for Prairie Lake, later renamed Lake Marion.

LAMBERT township (Red Lake County) is named for Francois Lambert of Quebec, an early settler who was the township treasurer for many years.

LAMBERTON city and township (Redwood County) honor Henry W. Lamberton, president of the Winona and Southwestern Railway and a state capitol commissioner.

LANESBORO city (Fillmore County) was probably named for the early settlers who came from Lanesboro Township in Massachusetts, though F. A. Lane was one of the stockholders in the original town site company, and the city may be named for him.

LANESBURG township (Le Sueur County) honors its first settler, Charles L. Lane, a farmer and postmaster.

LANGHEI township (Pope County) has a Norwegian name meaning "a long highland" and is one of the highest points of this county.

LANSING township (Mower County) is named for the capital of Michigan, though residents also intended it as a compliment to a pioneer settler, Alanson B. Vaughan, because of its similarity to his first name.

LAPORTE city (Hubbard County) has a name that in French means "the door or gate." After J. C. Stuart was appointed postmaster in 1900, the town was called Lake Port, but the mail was confused with Lake Park, so Mrs. Stuart named it for the Iowa town where she was married.

LAUDERDALE city (Ramsey County) was named for William H. Lauderdale, a veterinarian who had a dairy and real estate business in the area.

LEAF MOUNTAIN township (Otter Tail County) was named for its Leaf Hills or "mountains," a belt of morainic drift hills. The Ojibwe called them "Rustling Leaf Mountain," and two Leaf Lakes and the Leaf River are also named for the hills.

LEAVENWORTH township (Brown County) was probably named in honor of Henry Leavenworth, the military officer who founded Fort St. Anthony, which was later renamed Fort Snelling.

LE CENTER city (Le Sueur County) is the county seat; its name was changed in 1931 from Le Sueur Center to its present form, presumably in reference to its location at the center of the county.

LE CLAIRE village (Lake of the Woods County) is noted as the first truly American settlement in the county. The origin of its name is unknown, though the French word means "the clear" or "the clearing."

LEECH LAKE township (Cass County) was named for its lake, translated from the Ojibwe name, for the great number of leeches present in its waters.

LEO village (Roseau County) was named in honor of Pope Leo XIII, while St. Leo (Yellow Medicine County) was named for the first Pope Leo, also known as Leo the Great.

LEOTA township (Nobles County) is the only township, village, or physical feature in Nobles County named in honor of an Indian. Leota was a character in an Indian adventure story, and the name was given by Dutch settlers for their former home in Iowa.

LE SUEUR COUNTY and city and township commemorate a French Canadian trader and explorer, Pierre Charles Le Sueur, who explored the Minnesota River valley in the late seventeenth century.

LEWISVILLE city (Watonwan County) was named in honor of the Lewis brothers, Richard, James, and Nelson, who farmed here and whose father, Thomas, was the first settler. Richard was the first postmaster, and James was president of the Merchants' State Bank.

LEXINGTON city (Anoka County) was named at the suggestion of committee chair Leo Ryan, who noted that the area, bounded on the east by Lexington Avenue, had generally been known as Lexington Park. Ryan also wished to commemorate his army unit, the First Pioneer Infantry Regiment of Boston, which had fought the British in the Battle of Lexington.

LIGHTNING lake (Grant County) was named for a man who was killed by a lightning strike here, according to the famous guide Pierre Bottineau.

LILY lake (Waseca County) was named for its many white water lilies, while Lilly Lake (also Waseca County) commemorates an Irish immigrant, Terrence Lilly.

LIMA township (Cass County) was probably named for the city in Ohio, and its name is pronounced with the English long *i*.

LIME CITY village (Fillmore County) was named for the lime (calcium oxide) burned here.

LINCOLN COUNTY and townships (Blue Earth and Marshall Counties) were named for President Abraham Lincoln. The county's name was the fourth attempt by the state to honor him, the efforts in 1861, 1866, and 1870 having failed to garner the necessary support.

LIND township (Roseau County) was named in honor of John Lind, Minnesota's fourteenth governor.

LINDFORD township (Koochiching County) was named in part for its first postmaster, Andrew L. Lindvall. He suggested numerous names for the settlement, and the one chosen combines his name and that of automobile maker Henry Ford.

LINDSTROM city (Chisago County) was named for Swede Daniel Lindstrom, a pioneer farmer.

LINO LAKES city (Anoka County) was incorporated in 1955. In 1894, it was a farmers' post office called Lino, for what reason we do not know.

LINWOOD township (Anoka County) received its name from the lake. The name refers to the lin tree or linden; the American species is commonly called basswood.

LITCHFIELD city and township (Meeker County) were named in honor of a prominent family, including three brothers, Egbert, Edwin, and Darwin, who aided in the construction and financing of the St. Paul and Pacific Railroad here. The city is the county seat.

LITOMYSL village (Steele County) received its name from a town in western Bohemia (now the Czech Republic), the former home of many of its early settlers.

LITTLE CANADA city and township (Ramsey County) were originally known as New Canada and were probably named by first settler Benjamin Gervais, a French Canadian farmer, voyageur, and trader who arrived in 1844.

LITTLE CHICAGO trading post (Clearwater County) earned its name as an area famous for bootleg liquor.

LITTLE FALLS city and township (Morrison County) received their name from Zebulon Pike, who called the falls of the Mississippi River here "Painted Rock or Little Falls." The city is the county seat.

LITTLE MARAIS village (Lake County) was named by French voyageurs for its little marsh, in contrast with the larger marsh of Grand Marais in Cook County.

LIVONIA township (Sherburne County) may be named for Livonia Spencer, who served as probate judge of the county. It is also the name of a region in Russia.

LODI township (Mower County) takes its name from the city in Lombardy, Italy, made famous by a victory at its bridge by Napoleon against the Austrians in 1796.

LOGAN township (Grant County) commemorates John A. Logan, a congressman from Illinois, general in the Civil War, and U.S. senator, while another township (Aitkin County) was named for the long and narrow lakes found in abandoned channels of the Mississippi River, known as "logans."

LONE TREE township (Chippewa County) received its name for a solitary tall cottonwood tree near the west end of Bad Water or Lone Tree Lake, a landmark for early immigrants to this county.

LONG LAKE townships (Crow Wing, Itasca, and Watonwan Counties) are each named for a lake in the area, translated from the Ojibwe name. There are over fifty lakes with this name scattered throughout the state.

LONG PRAIRIE city and township (Todd County) take their name from the river that flows through the county to the Crow Wing River. The river was named for a narrow prairie that borders its east side for twenty miles. The city is the county seat.

LOONEYVILLE village (Houston County) was first settled by John S. Looney; the village takes his name, and that's no joke.

LORETTO city (Hennepin County) was named for a Catholic mission for refugees of the Huron Indians near Quebec, Canada, called Lorette, and for the village of Loretto, Ky., where the Catholic Sisters of Loretto at the Foot of the Cross was founded in 1812, both of which took their names from Loreto, a shrine in Italy.

LOST creek (Fillmore County) appears to be missing because it flows through creviced limestone beds underground for two miles.

LUCAN city (Redwood County) was named for a city near Dublin, Ireland. Another version of its name is that one of the railroad surveyors was named Lou Kartak, and when another surveyor was asked if he could think of a name for the town, he replied, "No, but maybe Lou can."

LUCKNOW village (St. Louis County) was named for a city in India where British soldiers made a heroic defense against mutineers in 1857.

LUTSEN township (Cook County) was named for a town in Prussian Saxony, made memorable by a 1632 battle where Gustavus Adolphus, king of Sweden, lost his life.

LUVERNE city and township (Rock County) were named in honor of Eva Luverne Hawes, the eldest daughter of the first settler here, Philo Hawes. The city is the county seat.

LYND city and township (Lyon County) were named for an early fur trader, James W. Lynd, who studied Dakota language and customs.

LYON COUNTY was named in honor of Gen. Nathaniel Lyon, who was killed in the Civil War battle of Wilson's Creek, Mo., on August 10, 1861.

LYRA township (Blue Earth County) has a name from ancient mythology, originally used to designate a northern constellation that resembled the lyre carried by Apollo.

MACSVILLE township (Grant County) was named in honor of three Macs—Francis McNabb, John McQuillan, and Coll McClellan—early settlers who served as chairman of the first board of supervisors, first township clerk, and chairman of the board of county commissioners, respectively.

MADELIA city and township (Watonwan County) are named in honor of the daughter of Gen. Madeline Hartshorn, one of the town site proprietors.

MADISON city and township (Lac qui Parle County) take the name from Madison, Wis., as suggested by early settler Claus P. Moe, for his former home. The city is the county seat.

MADISON LAKE city (Blue Earth County) was named for its adjoining lake, which had been named in honor of James Madison, fourth president of the United States.

MAHNOMEN COUNTY and city, the county seat, are named with one of the various spellings of the Ojibwe word for wild rice, which is plentiful in the area. Mahnomen County comprises half the area of the White Earth Reservation.

MAHTOMEDI city (Washington County) bears the Dakota name for White Bear Lake. *See* White Bear Lake

MAMRE township (Kandiyohi County) took the name of the nearby lake, which John Rodman, one of the first settlers, named for the biblical reference in Genesis to the home of Abraham in the Promised Land.

MANFRED township (Lac qui Parle County) is named for the main character in a wild and weird dramatic poem by Lord Byron.

MANITOU township (Koochiching County) received this Ojibwe name meaning "spirit" from the nearby Manitou Rapids of Rainy River. The name is also shared by the Manitou River (Lake County).

MANKATO city and township (Blue Earth County) take their name from the Dakota word for Blue Earth, *mahkato*. The city is the county seat.

MANTORVILLE city and township (Dodge County) honor three brothers, Peter, Riley, and Frank Mantor, who settled here in 1853. The city is the county seat.

MANTRAP township and lake (Hubbard County) and Little Man Trap Lake (Clearwater County) are named because many peninsulas and tamarack swamps at the head of their bays baffled or trapped hunters who attempted to pass around them.

MANY POINT lake (Becker County) has a name translated from the aboriginal name, referring to the many bays and intervening points of the shore.

MANYASKA township and lake (Martin County) bear a Dakota name probably meaning "white bank or bluff" or perhaps "white iron": *maza*, iron, and *ska*, white. *See* Mazaska

MAPLE LAKE city and township (Wright County) have the name of their largest lake, which not surprisingly is surrounded by sugar maple trees.

MAPLE PLAIN city and **MAPLE GROVE** township (Hennepin County) were named for the abundance of sugar maples in their forests.

MAPLEWOOD city (Ramsey County) has long worked to preserve its scenic woodlands and prairies, from which its name is likely derived, while the township (Otter Tail County) was named for its abundant sugar maple trees.

MARBLE city (Itasca County) likely took its name from the Gross-Marble Mining Company, while the township (Lincoln County) was named for its pale yellowish limestone boulders, some of which resemble marble in hardness.

MARION township (Olmsted County) shares its name with places in twenty-five other states, honoring Francis Marion of South Carolina, a distinguished general during the Revolutionary War.

MARSHALL COUNTY and city and lake (Lyon County) and township (Mower County) were named for Gov. William R. Marshall. Marshall served as a colonel in the Seventh Minnesota Regiment during the Civil War and as governor from 1866 to 1870. The city is the county seat.

MARSHFIELD township (Lincoln County) commemorates two pioneer settlers, Charles Marsh and Ira Field.

MARTIN COUNTY may have been named in honor of Henry Martin, a Connecticut businessman who purchased 2,000 acres of land in the counties of Mower, Fill-

more, and Brown, a portion of which was set apart as
Martin County. Another candidate for the honor is Morgan Lewis Martin, who as a congressional delegate from
Wisconsin Territory introduced a bill to organize Minnesota Territory in 1846. A township (Rock County) is
named for its first settler, John Martin.

MARYSVILLE township (Wright County) was named by
its early Roman Catholic settlers in honor of the mother
of Jesus.

MAUDADA village (Traverse County) is named for Maud
and Ada, respectively the daughters of A. C. Earsley and
Charles F. Washburn, platters of the village in 1888.

MAY township (Washington County) was named for
early landowner and farmer Morgan May while another
township (Cass County) commemorates May Griffith,
daughter of a county auditor.

MAYHEW LAKE township (Benton County) was named
for its lake and creek, which honor George V. Mayhew, a
state representative and officer in the Seventh Minnesota Regiment during the Civil War.

MAYNARD city (Chippewa County) was named by John
M. Spicer, superintendent of this division of the Great
Northern Railway, in honor of his sister's husband.

MAZASKA lake (Rice County) took its name from a
Dakota word for "white iron," or silver. *See* Manyaska

MAZEPPA city and township (Wabasha County) are
named for Ivan Mazeppa, a Cossack chief commemorated in a poem by Lord Byron.

McGREGOR city and township (Aitkin County) honor either a trapper named McGregor or Maj. John G. MacGregor of Minneapolis.

McKINLEY townships (Cass and Kittson Counties) were named in honor of President William McKinley, who died from an assassin's bullet on September 14, 1901. The city (St. Louis County) was named for the mine developed by the McKinley brothers, John, William, and Duncan.

McLEOD COUNTY was named in honor of Martin McLeod, a pioneer fur trader and member of the territorial legislature. The name is pronounced as if spelled *McLoud*.

McPHERSON township (Blue Earth County) is named for Gen. James B. McPherson, a hero of the battle of Vicksburg who died during the Civil War.

MEDFORD city and township (Steele County) were named for early settler William K. Colling's son, who in turn was named for the ship on which he was born.

MEDICINE LAKE city and township (Hennepin County) are located on a peninsula of the lake from which they take their name, a translation from the Indian name, which more correctly means "mysterious lake." An Indian drowned here when his canoe capsized during a sudden storm, and members of his tribe attributed powers to the lake because they could not locate his body.

MEDICINE WOOD camping area (Washington County) is located on the west end of Gray Cloud Island and took its name from a large beech tree, which the native population believed was placed here by the Great Spirit and held the power to protect or punish them as appropriate.

MEDINA township and lake (Hennepin County) take their name from the city in Arabia where Mohammed spent his last ten years. The name was the unanimous selection of the thirty-seven settlers, who for unknown reasons changed the town name from its earlier one: Hamburg.

MEDO township (Blue Earth County) is named with the Dakota word *mdo*, for a species of wild potato.

MEEKER COUNTY was named in honor of Bradley B. Meeker, an associate justice of the territorial court from 1849 to 1853.

MELROSE city and township (Stearns County) were named either for the city in Scotland or by Warren Adley in honor of Melissa (or Melvina) and Rose, who may have been his daughters.

MENAHGA city (Wadena County) bears the Ojibwe name for the blueberry, spelled *meenahga* by Henry W. Longfellow in *The Song of Hiawatha*.

MENDOTA city and township (Dakota County) began as a trading post in 1812, the first Euro-American settlement in Minnesota. *Mendota* is a Dakota name meaning "the mouth of a river," and here the Minnesota River joins the Mississippi.

MENTOR city (Polk County) was named for a city in northeastern Ohio that was the vacation home of James Garfield during his final few years. Whether Garfield was a "mentor" for the townspeople here is unclear.

MERTON township (Steele County) was probably named for the township in Wisconsin. Merton is also the name of a village in England, home to a famous Augustinian abbey during the Middle Ages.

MESABI iron range (Cook, Itasca, and Lake Counties) has an Ojibwe name, defined as both "Giant Mountain" and "a very big stout man."

MIDWAY township (Cottonwood County) is named in reference to its location on the railroad, equidistant from St. Paul and Sioux City.

MILACA city (Mille Lacs County) is the county seat, and its name is shortened from the French *mille lacs,* meaning "thousand lakes."

MILAN city (Chippewa County) is named for the city in northern Italy.

MILBURN village (Pine County) was named for a local disaster: the destruction of a lumber mill by fire in 1894.

MILDRED village (Cass County) was named in honor of Mildred Scofield, the first postmaster.

MILLE LACS COUNTY and lake were named by the French, meaning "thousand lakes." The Dakota called the lake *Mde Wakan*—Wonderful Lake or Spirit Lake—while the Ojibwe name meant "Everywhere Lake" or "Great Lake." The lake is about 200 square miles, and the region itself has numerous smaller lakes.

MILOMA village (Jackson County) was named by putting together the first three letters of the railroads popularly known as the Milwaukee Road and the Omaha Railway.

MILROY city (Redwood County) was named for Maj. Gen. Robert H. Milroy, a Civil War officer.

MILTONA city and township (Douglas County) receive their name from the large lake, named for Mrs. Florence Miltona Roadruck, who with her husband homesteaded at its west end.

MINERVA township and lake (Clearwater County) take their name from the Roman goddess of wisdom.

MINNEAPOLIS city—the state's largest—and township (Hennepin County) have a name compounded from *Minne*, Dakota for "water," and *polis*, Greek for "city," meaning "city of lakes." The city is the county seat.

MINNEHAHA FALLS waterfall (Hennepin County) takes the Indian name meaning "laughing waters," popularized by Henry W. Longfellow's *The Song of Hiawatha*.

MINNEISKA city (Winona County) and township (Wabasha County) are named from the Whitewater River, which is a translation of its Dakota name: *Minne* for water, and *ska* for white.

MINNEOLA township (Goodhue County) has a name from the Dakota language meaning "much water."

MINNEOPA village (Blue Earth County) was named for the falls in nearby Minneopa Creek. Minneopa is a contraction of a Dakota word meaning "follows the water, two waterfalls."

MINNEOTA city (Lyon County) and township (Jackson County) have a Dakota name meaning "much water." The city was first known as Pumpa, designated by early Norwegian settlers because of the railroad water pump.

The changed name, however, refers to the abundance of water that flowed into an early settler's well. The township was named for the adjoining Spirit Lake and Lake Okoboji in northwest Iowa.

MINNESOTA river is the largest wholly contained in the state, and its name is Dakota for "sky-tinted water": *Minne,* water, and *sota,* somewhat clouded. Minnesota Lake township (Faribault County) is named for the nearby lake.

MINNETONKA city, township, and large adjoining lake (Hennepin County) were named by Gov. Alexander Ramsey, who created a compound from two Dakota words, *Minne,* meaning "water," and *tonka,* meaning "big or great": "the big water."

MINNETRISTA city and township (Hennepin County) are named with a word said to mean "crooked water," for the town's numerous odd-shaped lakes. While *Minne,* for water, is of Dakota derivation, *trista* is not found in either the Dakota or the Ojibwe languages. The name is an example of words coined by white settlers as if used by Indians.

MINNEWASKA township (Pope County) bears the name of the largest lake in the county, which was named with two Dakota words: *Minne,* water, and *washta,* good.

MISSISSIPPI river bears the name given by the Ojibwe meaning "great river" in the Algonquian language. It flows from Lake Itasca (Clearwater County) to the Gulf of Mexico and is the chief river of North America.

MIZPAH city (Koochiching County) is named with the Hebrew word for a watchtower, as found in Genesis:

"The Lord watch between me and thee, when we are absent one from another."

MOLLY STARK lake (Otter Tail County) was named for the wife of John Stark, a noted general of the Revolutionary War who won the battle of Bennington, August 16, 1777.

MOLTKE township (Sibley County) was named by its German pioneers in honor of the Prussian general, Count Helmuth von Moltke (1800–1891).

MONEY CREEK township (Houston County) was named for the creek here, which was in turn named after a man got his pocketbook and contents wet in the creek and spread out the bank notes on a bush to dry. A sudden gust of wind blew them into the water again, and some of the notes were never recovered.

MONTEVIDEO city (Chippewa County) is the county seat and may have taken its name from the Latin phrase signifying "from the mountain I see" or "Mount of Vision," but more likely was named for the capital of Uruguay.

MONTGOMERY city and township (Le Sueur County) are probably named for Gen. Richard Montgomery, who in the American Revolution commanded an expedition invading Canada during which he was killed on December 31, 1775.

MONTICELLO city and township (Wright County) do not take their name from Thomas Jefferson's home but rather from what one of the township proprietors called "the Little Mountain," a modest hill about two miles southeast of the village.

MOONSHINE township (Big Stone County) never figured in the manufacture of illicit liquor, but rather takes its name from its lake, which an early settler intended to call Moon Lake, for the surname of his wife. Bright moonlight led to the more descriptive name.

MOORHEAD city and township (Clay County) are named in honor of William G. Moorhead of Pennsylvania, a director of the Great Northern Railway and a partner of financier Jay Cooke. The city is the county seat.

MOOSE LAKE city and township (Carlton County) are named for their Moose Lake and Moose Head Lake, which likely carry translations of their original Ojibwe names. Another township (Beltrami County) was similarly named, for a different Moose Lake and for Little Moose Lake.

MOOSEVILLE village (Chippewa County) received this name for unknown reasons (though we can guess), but the village was for a time also known as Dead Man Corner because of a 1930s automobile accident that killed four people.

MORA city and lake (Kanabec County) were named by Israel Israelson for his hometown in Sweden. The city is the county seat.

MORRIS city (Stevens County) is the county seat and was named in honor of Charles A. F. Morris, who was connected with the engineering departments of several railroads.

MORRISON COUNTY was named in honor of William and Allan Morrison, fur traders from Quebec who had trading posts in northern Minnesota.

MORRISTOWN city, township, and lake (Rice County) were named in honor of settler and preacher Jonathan Morris.

MOSCOW township (Freeborn County) was named because of a forest fire many years prior to settlement. The flames reminded spectators of scenes in Russia under Napoleon, and the burned trees became known as Moscow timber, from which the town was named.

MOUND city (Hennepin County) is named for the three groups of aboriginal mounds within the area of the original village. The township (Rock County) contains a large plateau of rock that was called "the Mound" by settlers and for which Rock County and River were named.

MOUNDS VIEW city and township (Ramsey County) have a tract of hills that offer a fine panoramic view from their northern and highest points.

MOUNTAIN IRON city (St. Louis County) was named for its Mountain Iron Mine, the first to ship ore from the Mesabi Range, in 1892.

MOUNTAIN LAKE city and township (Cottonwood County) derived their name from the large lake and its forty-foot mountain-like island with steep shores and a nearly flat top.

MOWER COUNTY commemorates John E. Mower, lumberman and representative to the state legislature.

MUD LAKE township (Cass County) is named for the nearby shallow, muddy lake, but the name is shared with more than fifty lakes in Minnesota, all named, presumably, for their turbid waters.

MUNCH township (Pine County) honors the three Munch brothers, Adolph, Emil, and Paul, natives of Prussia who were lumbermen in the county. Emil later became a state representative and state treasurer, and Paul served as a lieutenant in the Civil War.

MURRAY COUNTY and township take the name of William P. Murray, an Ohio lawyer who moved to Minnesota and was a member of the state constitutional convention and a state senator.

MUSTINKA river (Grant County) is named with a Dakota word for rabbit. This species is also called the "varying hare" because its fur is gray in summer and white in winter.

MYSTERY CAVE state park (Fillmore County) has the state's largest known limestone cave, which contains twelve miles of passageways. How it got its name is, well, a mystery.

NAGONAB railroad station (St. Louis County) bears the name of an Ojibwe leader of the Fond du Lac band in the nineteenth century, translated as "Sitting Ahead."

NASHUA city (Wilkin County) was named for its Nash families but matches the spelling of a city and river in New Hampshire and a village in Iowa, whose name means "land between."

NASHWAUK city and township (Itasca County) have an Algonquin name, from the Nashwaak River and village, near Fredericton, New Brunswick. The meaning is likely similar to that of Nashua.

NAY-TAH-WAUSH village (Mahnomen County) is named with words meaning "smooth sailing." In 1906 the town for unknown reasons changed its name from Twin Lakes.

NEBISH township and lake (Beltrami County) are named with a shortened version of the Ojibwe word *anibish*, for a tea enjoyed by both natives and settlers.

NELSON city (Douglas County) honors Knute Nelson, a prominent citizen of the county who served as state congressman and governor before becoming a U.S. senator.

NEMADJI village (Carlton County) has the Ojibwe name for the river, meaning "Left Hand River." The name refers to its location on the left side when one passes from Lake Superior into the St. Louis River.

NERSTRAND city (Rice County) was named by its platter, Osmund Osmundson, for his former home in Norway.

NET rivers or creeks (Carlton County) are probably translated from their Ojibwe names, referring to nets for catching fish.

NEVADA township (Mower County) received its name from the Sierra Nevada, or "Snowy Range," in eastern California.

NEVIS city and township (Hubbard County) were named either for Scotland's Ben Nevis, the highest mountain of Great Britain, or for the island in the West Indies.

NEW BRIGHTON city (Ramsey County) got its start as a stockyard and meat packing operation and took its name from Brighton, Mass., formerly an important cattle market.

NEW GERMANY city (Carver County) compliments the many German settlers in its vicinity. During World War I, the name was temporarily changed to Motordale because of popular sentiment against Germany.

NEW HOPE city (Hennepin County) was incorporated in 1953, but the origin of its name is uncertain. Perhaps the "old hope" had worn off.

NEW LONDON city and township (Kandiyohi County) were named by Louis Larson for his former home, a "prospering village" in Wisconsin, itself likely named for the already prosperous city in England.

NEW MARKET city and township (Scott County) are thought to have adopted this name from the town near Cambridge, England, famous for its horse races.

NEW PRAGUE city (Le Sueur and Scott Counties) was named for the ancient city of Prague, the capital of Bohemia (now the Czech Republic), from which many settlers immigrated.

NEW ULM city (Brown County) is the county seat and was founded by German colonists who gave it the name of their former home in Germany.

NEW YORK MILLS city and township (Otter Tail County) were named for the New York Mills Company, which bought the township land and a sawmill from Randolph L. Frazee. After the company dissolved, Finnish immigrants developed the community.

NEWFOLDEN city and **NEW FOLDEN** township (Marshall County) were named for a seaport located on the Folden Fjord in Norway. The name was changed from the original, Baltic, given by the Soo Line for the numerous Baltic elevators along the line.

NEWPORT city and township (Washington County) were named by Mrs. James H. Hugunin, probably not as a shipping center but rather for a place by this name in one of thirty other states.

NICOLLET COUNTY and township were named in honor of Joseph Nicollet, geographer and explorer of Minnesota and the Dakotas and the first to make an accurate map of the area.

NIGGER HILL village (Lake County) was named for an engine used for hoisting materials.

NIMROD city (Wadena County) has a biblical name, for the grandson of Ham, who is in Genesis called "a mighty hunter before the Lord" and who is reputed to have directed the construction of the Tower of Babel.

NISSWA city (Crow Wing County) bears an Ojibwe name related to *nassawaii,* meaning "in the middle," probably due to its location at mid-lake.

NOBLES COUNTY was named for William H. Nobles, who was a member of the Minnesota territorial legislature in 1854 and 1856 and who advocated construction of a wagon road across southwestern Minnesota.

NODINE village (Winona County) was named, according to local story, by two government surveyors who could not find a place to eat.

NOKAY LAKE township (Crow Wing County) has the lake of this name and the Nokasippi or Nokay River. *Noka* was the name of an Ojibwe leader and noted hunter.

NORCROSS city (Grant County) has a name that combines those of Henry A. Norton and Judson N. Cross, who were proprietors of the original village site.

NORMAN COUNTY and city (Yellow Medicine County) and township (Pine County) received this name because the majority of their early settlers were Norwegians. A native of Norway is often referred to as *Norsk*, or Norman.

NORTH BRANCH city (Chisago County) and township (Isanti County) were named for their locations on the north branch of the Sunrise River.

NORTH HERO township (Redwood County) was named by Byron Knight for his old home, the island of North

Hero in Lake Champlain, Vt., which was named in honor of Ethan Allen, whose expeditions with the Green Mountain Boys during the Revolutionary War were legendary.

NORTH OAKS city (Ramsey County) was originally the hobby farm of railroad magnate James J. Hill. Incorporated in 1956, it is now a residential community.

NORTH POLE village (Beltrami County) exists, like Santa's home, only in our minds. It was proposed as a village in November 1940 to take advantage of the Christmas holiday, but Gov. Joseph A. A. Burnquist vetoed the proposal, and the town did not appear on a state highway tourist map the next year.

NORTH ST. PAUL city (Ramsey County) is northeast of St. Paul. It was originally named Castle in honor of Capt. Henry Anson Castle, who founded the community.

NORTH STAR township (Brown County) received its name in reference to the French motto *L'Etoile du Nord,* which appears on the state seal. Minnesota is often called the North Star State.

NORTHERN township (Beltrami County) is named for its location on Lake Bemidji.

NORTHFIELD city (Rice County) was named in honor of its principal founder, John W. North.

NORTHWEST ANGLE region (Lake of the Woods County) was named for its triangular shape and for its position north of the forty-ninth parallel, which makes it the most northern tract of the United States except for Alaska.

NOWHERE locality (Itasca County) was a logging site and, although never developed as a community, was referred to by name and "might as well have been in the middle of nowhere." It remains nowhere to this day.

NOWTHEN village (Anoka County) received its name by chance. When the village's clerk, James Hare, tried naming the community Burns and then Ada, he found that both names were already claimed. His use of English was idiosyncratic, and in both speaking and writing he began sentences with "Now then." After several more of his suggested names were rejected, he submitted one final scathing letter, concluding, "Now then, enough said." Officials responded, approving Nowthen.

NUNDA township (Freeborn County) was named by one of its early prominent citizens in honor of towns of the same name in New York and Illinois. It is an Indian word meaning "hilly" or "potato ground."

NUSHKA railroad station (Cass County) has an Ojibwe word of exclamation meaning "Look!" It was used by Henry W. Longfellow in *The Song of Hiawatha*.

OAK GROVE township (Anoka County) was named for the oak trees growing throughout the area.

OAK PARK HEIGHTS city (Washington County) was platted in 1938 and incorporated in 1959. Its name likely comes from the nearby Oak Park village site, which had originally been platted by John Parker as a residential community in 1857.

OAKDALE city and township (Washington County) were originally covered with white, black, and bur oak timber.

ODESSA township (Big Stone County) was named for the city in present-day Ukraine, which was the source of wheat seed used in this county, or for a girl named Dessa who died of diphtheria.

ODIN township (Watonwan County) bears the name of one of the chief gods in ancient Norse mythology. Odin was the source of wisdom and the patron of culture and of heroes.

OGEMA city (Becker County) is named with a word that in the Ojibwe language means "a chief."

OKABENA city (Jackson County) takes the Dakota name of the adjoining lake, meaning "nesting place of herons." Okaman (Waseca County) is similarly named.

OKLEE city (Red Lake County) bears the name of O. K. Lee, a Scandinavian settler on whose farm the village was built.

OLIVIA city (Renville County) is the county seat. There are two possibilities regarding the origin of its name: either the first railroad station agent in Ortonville was a woman named Olive, or the city was named for Margaret Olivia Sage, wife of an official of the Chicago, Milwaukee and St. Paul Railroad Company.

OLMSTED COUNTY was named in honor of David Olmsted, the first mayor of St. Paul and a trader and newspaper editor.

ONAMIA city and township (Mille Lacs County) bear the name of the third and largest of the three lakes through which the Rum River flows below the mouth of Mille Lacs. The name is from the Ojibwe, meaning "red lake."

ONEOTA village (St. Louis County) took its name from Henry Schoolcraft's book, published in 1845 and titled *Oneota, or Characteristics of the Red Race of America*. According to Schoolcraft, *Oneota* or *Oneida* is a Mohawk word meaning "the people who are sprung from a rock."

ORANGE township (Douglas County) is said to be named for Holland's William of Orange.

ORONO city and township (Hennepin County) were named for the town in Maine, which in turn commemorates the Penobscot leader of this name.

ORONOCO township (Olmsted County) was named, with a different spelling, for the large Orinoco River in South America, referring to the waterpower of the middle branch of the Zumbro River here.

ORROCK township (Sherburne County) was named in honor of Scottish immigrant Robert Orrock, the township's first settler.

ORTONVILLE city and township (Big Stone County) are named for Cornelius K. Orton, who platted the village. The city is the county seat.

OSAGE township (Becker County) and towns in five other states were named for the Osage Indian tribe.

OSAKIS city (Douglas and Todd Counties) received its name from the lake, which also has the Sauk River flowing from it. Each of these names refers to the Sauk (Sac) Indians.

OSCAR township (Otter Tail County) commemorates Oscar II, king of Sweden and Norway from 1872 until 1907.

OSCEOLA township (Renville County) was named by a county commissioner for the village in Wisconsin, which in turn honors a Seminole leader.

OSLO city (Marshall County) bears the name of the capital city of Norway.

OSSEO city (Hennepin County) takes its name from Henry W. Longfellow's *The Song of Hiawatha*, which recounts the story of Osseo, "son of the Evening Star."

OTENEAGEN township (Itasca County) was named by a lumberman for a river in Michigan, the Ontonagon. The name may mean "fishing place," but another account of the name recalls an Ojibwe woman losing a dish in a stream and exclaiming "nindonogan," which means "away goes my dish."

OTSEGO city and township (Wright County) were named for a lake, a township, and a county in New York.

The name is an Indian word meaning "welcome water" or "place where meetings are held."

OTTAWA township (Le Sueur County) is named for a tribe of the Algonquian family closely related to the Ojibwe.

OTTER TAIL COUNTY and city and township received their name from the lake and river. The lake's name comes from the Ojibwe, for a long and narrow sandbar that has an outline similar in shape to the tail of an otter.

OUTING resort town (Cass County) was registered in 1909 by William H. Andrews as a place for "outings" of city people and sportsmen who enjoyed the resorts on Lake Roosevelt.

OWATONNA city (Steele County) is the county seat and is named with the Dakota word for the Straight River, which many have noted is anything but.

OXFORD township (Isanti County) was named by early settlers for a village in Maine, which likely traces its name to the city and university in England. The name means "oxen's ford." *See also* Cambridge

PALISADE city (Aitkin County) was named by an official of the Soo Line railroad for the high embankment on either side of the Mississippi River.

PALMER township (Sherburne County) was originally named Briggs for early settler Joshua Briggs. The name was later changed to honor Dr. Robinson Palmer, Briggs's father-in-law. The nearby Briggs Lake still retains Joshua's name.

PALMYRA township (Renville County) was named by settlers who came from Palmyra, Wis. Sixteen other states also have villages and townships named for the ancient Syrian oasis city of Palmyra, the name meaning "city of palms."

PARK RAPIDS city (Hubbard County) is the county seat and was named for its park-like groves and prairies located beside the rapids of the Fish Hook River.

PARKE township (Clay County) was probably named to honor a pioneer settler, but three versions of the naming exist. One is that a man in an eastern state sent $50 to put a shingle on the school if they would rename the town, then known as Oak Grove, in his honor; a second is that it was named Park because of its park-like beauty, with the "e" added to honor an easterner who sent $50; and the third is that the original name was Parktown and a man named Parke gave $100 and asked that the name be changed to its present spelling.

PARTRIDGE township (Pine County) may have the name of one of its first settlers, though many residents believe it was named for the game bird indigenous to the area, which is true of the lake and river (St. Louis County). More likely, the township was named for a ridge that runs southwest to northeast, dividing or "parting" the township.

PAY lake (Kandiyohi County) was named because the paymaster for a railroad construction crew had his camp here.

PAYNESVILLE city and township (Stearns County) were named for Edwin E. Payne, who was the first settler and postmaster.

PEACE township (Kanabec County) was named by vote of its people, in direct contrast to its village of Warman.

PEACE ROCK formation (Benton County) was named by Henry Schoolcraft because, together with the Watab River, it marked part of the boundary line between the Ojibwe and the Dakota, agreed upon in the Treaty of 1825 at Prairie du Chien.

PEASE city (Mille Lacs County) was named by the railroad either for James J. Hill's friend, Granville S. Pease of Anoka, or as a misspelling of Peace, the name requested by town residents.

PELICAN RAPIDS city and **PELICAN** township and river (Otter Tail County) take their name from the Ojibwe, while another township (Crow Wing County) was named for its large Pelican Lake, which was frequented by these birds.

PEMBINA township (Mahnomen County) is named for the bush cranberry, called by the Ojibwe *nepin ninan,* meaning "summer berry." The Ojibwe words were transformed into this name by French voyageurs and traders.

PENASSE island (Lake of the Woods County) was named for Tom Penasse, a local Indian.

PENNINGTON COUNTY was named in honor of Edmund Pennington, a railroad executive with the Soo Line.

PEPIN lake (Goodhue and Wabasha Counties) is located on the Mississippi River and was probably named in honor of Pepin le Bref, a king of the Franks who was the father of Charlemagne.

PEPPERMINT creek (Lake of the Woods County) is named for its native species of mint, most notably the wild bergamot.

PEQUOT LAKES city (Crow Wing County) was named by a postal official with the first Indian-sounding name he thought of, which is the name of a former tribe of Algonquin Indians in eastern Connecticut.

PERHAM city and township (Otter Tail County) are named in honor of Josiah Perham, the first president of the Northern Pacific Railroad Company.

PERRY township (Lac qui Parle County) honors Oliver H. Perry, victor in the battle of Lake Erie, fought on September 10, 1813.

PETERSBURG township (Jackson County) was named for Rev. Peter Baker, a pioneer Methodist minister who settled in the township in 1860 and was its first postmaster.

PIERZ township (Morrison County) was named in honor of Father Francis Xavier Pierz, a Catholic missionary to the Indians and the German colonists in the county.

PIGEON river and falls (Cook County) have a name derived from the Ojibwe, in reference to the now-extinct passenger pigeon.

PIG'S EYE village, lake, island, and lighthouse (Ramsey County) were all named for Pierre "Pig's Eye" Parrant, a rogue and whiskey seller in pre-territorial times. His nickname called attention to his ill-appearing eye.

PIKE township (St. Louis County) and island (Dakota County) commemorate Lt. Zebulon Pike, commander of the expedition sent to the upper Mississippi in 1805–6, as do Pike Creek township (Morrison County), and Pike Bay township (Cass County).

PILLAGER city and lake (Cass County) are named for a robbery or pillage that occurred in 1767 or 1768, when a trader was relieved of his goods at the mouth of the Crow Wing River.

PILLSBURY city (Todd County) and township (Swift County) honor John S. Pillsbury, a lumber and flour executive who was governor from 1876 to 1882.

PILOT GROVE township and lake (Faribault County) were uniquely named because of a grove of native timber that provided a prairie landmark by which immigrants "piloted" their way west.

PINE COUNTY and city, the county seat, and Pine City township, Pine Lake township, and the lakes and river were named with reference to the extensive forests of white and red (Norway) pine originally in various parts

of this district. More than thirty lakes and rivers throughout the state are similarly named.

PINE ISLAND township (Goodhue County) was named by
an early settler for the solitary large white pine on a
small island in the middle branch of the Zumbro River.

PIPESTONE COUNTY and city, the county seat, are named
for the celebrated quarry of red pipestone or catlinite,
used by Indians for pipe bowls.

PLAINVIEW township (Wabasha County) is located in the
watershed of the Zumbro and Whitewater Rivers, in
"plain view" of the surrounding country.

PLANTAGENET lake (Hubbard County) was named by
Henry Schoolcraft for a line of English kings who
reigned from 1154 to 1399. Their name was derived
from the flowering broom (in Latin, *plantagenista*), chosen as a family emblem by Geoffrey, Count of Anjou,
whose son was Henry II, the first of the Plantagenet
kings.

PLUMMER city (Red Lake County) was named for Charles
A. Plummer, who built a sawmill and gristmill on the
Clearwater River near the site of this village around
1881.

PLYMOUTH city and township (Hennepin County) and
the many Plymouths in the United States commemorate
the city located at the mouth of the River Plym in Dev-
onshire, England, where the Pilgrims departed in the
Mayflower.

POKEGAMA townships (Itasca and Pine Counties) are
named for the irregularly shaped lake, its name translated from the Ojibwe as "the water which juts off from

another water" or "lake with bays branching out."
Pokegama Falls, on the Mississippi River, is also named
for this lake.

POLK COUNTY was named in honor of President James K.
Polk. On March 3, 1849, his next-to-last day as president, he approved the act creating Minnesota Territory.

POMME DE TERRE township (Grant County) took the
name of the large lake at its southeast border, from
which flows the Pomme de Terre River. The name is
French, meaning literally "apple of the earth," or potato,
but actually refers to the wild turnip, a valuable food
source for the Dakota.

PONEMAH village (Beltrami County) bears a name used
by Henry W. Longfellow in *The Song of Hiawatha*.

POPE COUNTY was named in honor of John Pope, an explorer who traveled from Fort Snelling up the Mississippi and Sauk Rivers to the Red River. He served as a
general during the Civil War.

POPPLE township (Clearwater County) and Popple
Grove township (Mahnomen County) were named for
their plentiful poplar woods, commonly misspelled and
mispronounced, as in this name. Similarly, Poppleton
township (Kittson County) received its name for the
plentiful poplar trees and groves in the area. Originally
Poplartown, common mispronunciation changed the
name to Poppleton.

PORTER city (Yellow Medicine County) was named for
the L. C. Porter Milling Company, which erected the
city's first grain warehouse.

POTOSI post office (Stevens County) has a name that means "great riches," though in what language we are uncertain.

PRAIRIE ISLAND Indian reservation (Goodhue County) is named for the island, a translation from the French *Isle Peleé*.

PRAIRIE VIEW township (Wilkin County) has from its high eastern part an extensive view over the flat Red River Valley.

PRESTON city and township (Fillmore County) were named by mill owner John Kaercher in honor of his millwright, Luther Preston. This "founding father" was not always honorable: Preston was appointed the first postmaster but was convicted of theft in 1859. The city is the county seat.

PRINCETON city and township (Mille Lacs and Sherburne Counties) were named in honor of John S. Prince of St. Paul, one of the platters of this village in 1855, a trader, banker, and mayor of St. Paul.

PRINSBURG city (Kandiyohi County) in Holland Township was named in honor of Martin Prins, member of a land firm in the Netherlands who came here in 1884 and acquired about 35,000 acres of railroad land, mostly in this county, on which many Dutch families settled.

PRIOR LAKE city (Scott County) has the name of its lake, which honors Charles H. Prior, a long-time superintendent of the Minnesota divisions of the Chicago, Milwaukee and St. Paul Railroad.

PROCTOR city (St. Louis County) commemorates J. Proctor Knott, who delivered to Congress in 1871 a riotously funny speech in which he ridiculed Duluth. It was a satirical speech, but residents of a Duluth suburb rewarded him by naming their town for him.

PULASKI township (Morrison County) and lake (Wright County) were named in honor of the Polish general Casimir Pulaski, who aided George Washington during the Revolutionary War.

PUPOSKY village and lake (Beltrami County) are named with an Ojibwe word signifying "the end of the shaking lands," that is, a swamp whose surface sinks when walked on, or a bog.

QUADNA township (Aitkin County) has a name shortened from *Piquadinaw*, an Ojibwe term referring to the
tracts of knolls and hilly drifts extending east from the
high hill of this name.

QUAMBA city (Kanabec County) was first known as Mud
Creek, but railroad officials chose to use an Indian word
they defined as "mudhole" instead.

QUEEN township (Polk County) is named in relation to
the township to its west: King.

QUIRING township (Beltrami County) was supposedly
named during the township's organizational meeting
when an argument over the town's name ensued. Call-
ing for order, someone shouted, "Let us be quiet and
stop quarreling," causing another of the organization to
coin the town's name from the words "quiet" and "quarreling."

RADIUM village (Marshall County) was named for the metallic element radium, discovered in 1902.

RAIL PRAIRIE township (Morrison County) was named in honor of Case Rail, a pioneer farmer whose homestead was mostly prairie land.

RAINY lake (Koochiching and St. Louis Counties) and river (Koochiching and Lake of the Woods Counties) have translations from their aboriginal and early French names. *Ouchichiq* or *Koochiching* were names given to the river by the Cree and adopted by the Ojibwe. The explorer Joseph la France, traveling here in 1740, noted the derivation of the name *Lac de la Pluie,* which in English means "Lake of the Rain," from the mist of the falls of Rainy River at the site of today's International Falls. *See* Koochiching

RAMSEY COUNTY and city (Anoka County) and the state park and lake (Redwood County) honor Alexander Ramsey, the first governor of Minnesota Territory and later governor of the state, U.S. senator, and secretary of war.

RAPIDAN township (Blue Earth County) was named by a Civil War veteran for the river in Virginia. This name is also given to rapids and a dam on the Blue Earth River in the northwest part of the township.

RAT ROOT township, lake, and river (Koochiching County) bear a translation of the Ojibwe name, referring to the water lily roots eaten by muskrats.

RAVENNA township (Dakota County) was named by Albert T. Norton for the Ohio town where his wife had taught school.

READING village (Nobles County) is named not for Reading, Pa., but for a pioneer farmer named Henry H. Read.

READS LANDING village (Wabasha County) was named for Charles R. Read, who operated a trading post here beginning in 1847.

RED river (Kittson, Marshall, Polk, Norman, Clay, and Wilkin Counties) is named for Red Lake and is the boundary of Minnesota at the west side of six counties. Its more distinctive name, Red River of the North, was used by Joseph Nicollet to distinguish it from the Red River tributary to the lower Mississippi.

RED EYE township (Wadena County) is traversed by the Redeye River, named in translation from the Ojibwe for its red-eyed fish, the rock bass.

RED LAKE COUNTY and **RED LAKE FALLS** city, the county seat, were named for the river that flows through the city and county, translated from the Ojibwe and referring to water reddened through bloody battles or to reddish silt stirred up by storms or, most likely, to the sunset reflected upon the water. There are many similarly named lakes and rivers throughout the state.

RED ROCK village (Washington County) took its name from a rounded granite boulder, about five feet in length, which was held in great esteem by the Dakota. Similarly, the township (Mower County) was named by a settler from Rock County, Wis., for a red rock in the grove near his farm.

RED WING city (Goodhue County) is the county seat and is named for a succession of leaders of the Mdewakanton Dakota who resided on the west shore of Lake Pepin, where the city now stands. The name comes from the red-dyed swan's wing the men carried.

REDTOP town site (Aitkin County) takes its name either from the nickname of a local red-haired girl or from the redtop field grass that grows in the area.

REDWOOD COUNTY and **REDWOOD FALLS** city, the county seat, were named for the river, translated from the Dakota for the red willow. Other variations of the name's origin are for red cedars or for spots of red paint used to mark trees along a path.

REFORMATORY railroad station (Sherburne County) takes its name from the nearby St. Cloud Reformatory.

REGAL city (Kandiyohi County) earned its name when an early settler suggested three automobile names: Regal, because he owned one; Ford, because a local farmer had one; and Harvard, because it was a solid name. Regal won.

REMER city and township (Cass County) were named for brothers E. N. and William P. Remer, treasurer and manager of the Reishus-Remer Land Company and first postmaster, respectively.

RENO township (Pope County) was named for its large lake, which commemorates Jesse Lee Reno, a Civil War major general from West Virginia who was killed in the battle of South Mountain, Md.

RENVILLE COUNTY and city were named for Joseph Renville, son of a French father and an Indian mother who served as the interpreter for Maj. Stephen H. Long's expedition to the Red River and Lake Winnipeg in 1823.

RESERVE township (Ramsey County) had been part of the Fort Snelling military reservation until 1853. Its northern boundary coincided with the present Iglehart Avenue of St. Paul, and the township is now a suburb of the city.

REVERE city (Redwood County) was named in honor of Paul Revere, renowned for his ride from Boston to Lexington, April 18–19, 1775.

RICE COUNTY was named for Henry M. Rice, one of the first two U.S. senators from Minnesota. The many Rice Lakes, Rice Rivers, or Wild Rice bodies of water in Minnesota are named for the wild grain, translated from the Ojibwe *manomin* or *mahnomen*.

RICHFIELD city and township (Hennepin County) were named by a vote of residents in 1858, changing from the previous name, Richland, both names likely referring to fertile farmland.

RICHMOND city (Stearns County) was named for an early settler and also commemorates Reuben Richardson, who platted the original village. The township (Winona County) was named for a French lumber dealer.

RICHVILLE city and **RICHDALE** village (Otter Tail County) are named for Watson W. Rich, a civil engineer who served as a captain in the Fourth Minnesota Regiment during the Civil War.

RIDGELY township (Nicollet County) took its name from the fort, which was named by secretary of war Jefferson Davis in honor of three army officers from Maryland who died in the Mexican War: Lt. Henderson Ridgely, Capt. Randolph Ridgely, and Capt. Thomas P. Ridgely.

RIPLEY lake (Meeker County) commemorates Dr. Frederick N. Ripley, who froze to death here during the winter of 1855–56.

ROBBINSDALE city (Hennepin County) was named for Andrew B. Robbins, who purchased lands here in 1877 and platted the village.

ROCHESTER city (Olmsted County) is the county seat and was named by "the father of Rochester," George Head, for the city in New York, because the rapids of the Zumbro River reminded him of the waterpower near his previous home. Rochester is often called "the Queen City."

ROCK COUNTY and river refer to a prominent outcrop of reddish-gray quartzite that occupies an area of three or four square miles, rising to a height of 175 feet, the name translated from the Dakota, now known as "the Mound." The township (Pipestone County) is named for its location at the head of the river.

ROCKFORD township (Hennepin and Wright Counties) had an early sawmill, built at a ford of the Crow River that was strewn with boulders, leading to this appropriate name.

ROLETTE village (Norman County) commemorates Joe Rolette, a representative in the territorial legislature of Minnesota and a member of the territorial council. In 1857 he hid the bill to move the seat of government to St. Peter, thus saving the state capital for St. Paul.

ROLLINGSTONE city and township (Winona County) are named for the river, which takes its name from the Dakota for "the stream where the stone rolls."

ROOSEVELT city (Lake of the Woods and Roseau Counties) and townships (Beltrami and Crow Wing Counties) were named in honor of President Theodore Roosevelt.

ROOT river (Mower, Olmsted, Fillmore, and Houston Counties) has a name translated from the Dakota. *See* Hokah

ROSE DELL township (Rock County) bears a name suggested by a rocky gorge filled with beautiful wild roses.

ROSE HILL township (Cottonwood County) is named for its plentiful wild prairie roses and its low ridges and hills of morainic drift.

ROSEAU COUNTY and city, the county seat, are named from the lake and river. *Roseau* is French for "reeds," which grow abundantly in the shallow water of Minnesota and Manitoba's prairie region.

ROSEBUD township (Polk County) was named either for the abundance of wild roses in the area or for Rose Eikens, the first white child born in the settlement.

ROSEMOUNT city and township (Dakota County) received their name from two Irishmen recalling a picturesque village in Ireland.

ROSEVILLE city and **ROSE** township (Ramsey County) were named for Isaac Rose, a local landowner.

ROTHSAY city (Otter Tail and Wilkin Counties) was named by officers of a railway company for Rothesay, a seaport near Glasgow, Scotland.

ROWENA village (Redwood County) has the name of a character from Sir Walter Scott's novel *Ivanhoe*.

ROYALTON city (Morrison County) was named by settlers from Royalton, Vt., while the township (Pine County) was named for early settler Royal C. Gray.

RUM river (Mille Lacs, Isanti, Sherburne, and Anoka Counties) was originally named with the Dakota word for Mille Lacs, which translated as "Spirit Water" or "Spirit Lake." However, settlers changed the name to refer to the common "spirituous liquor" brought into the region by traders.

RUNEBERG township (Becker County) commemorates Johan L. Runeberg, a famous nineteenth-century Swedish poet.

RUSH city (Chisago County) was originally a railroad depot on the Rush River, named for the bulrushes along its banks. Over a dozen lakes and rivers of the same name can be found throughout the state.

RUSHFORD city and township (Fillmore County) take their name from Rush Creek, and the name was the unanimous selection of the nine pioneer settlers who voted on Christmas Day, 1854. The creek is surrounded by rushes that provide food for animals throughout the winter.

RUSHMORE city (Nobles County) has nothing to do with the famous Mount Rushmore in South Dakota, but rather is named for one of its pioneer merchants, S. M. Rushmore.

RUSHSEBA township (Chisago County) is in part an Ojibwe name, *seba* or *sippi* meaning "a river." Both Rush Lake and Rush River are translations from the aboriginal name.

S

SACRAMENTO village (Dodge County) received its name from the California city, in reference to traces of gold found near here on branches of the Zumbro and Root Rivers. Panning wasn't worth the effort, however, and this village is now deserted.

SACRED HEART city and township (Renville County) were settled mostly by Lutherans, so the adoption of a name of apparent Roman Catholic origins seems surprising. However, the name was derived from one given by the Dakota to an early trader, Charles Patterson. He wore a bearskin hat, and, because the bear was a sacred animal to the Indians, they called him the "Sacred Hat" man, which gradually became Sacred Heart.

SAGANAGA lake (Cook County) takes a name that has been translated a number of different ways. The Ojibwe word may mean "numerous islands" or "lake surrounded by thick forests." Though similar in sound, this place name is probably not related to Michigan's Saginaw County, city, and river.

SAGO township (Itasca County) was named at the suggestion of a county commissioner after a sago pudding was served at dinner, or it may be a contraction of Saginaw, Mich., the former home of many of the early loggers of the region.

SAHLINARK post office (Stevens County) was misspelled when it was registered. It should have been Sahlmark, for Charles A. Sahlmark, a farmer and postmaster.

ST. ANTHONY city (Hennepin County) and **ST. ANTHONY PARK** district (Ramsey County) share their name with St. Anthony Falls, named by Louis Hennepin for his patron saint, Anthony of Padua, a twelfth-century Franciscan friar.

ST. AUGUSTA township (Stearns County) has a history of name changes, beginning as Berlin in 1859 and later changing to Neenah. In 1863 it took the name St. Augusta from the first church here, also honoring the village's platter, Augusta Wilson, and his daughter, who died at a young age. The village was not incorporated until 2000, and then under the name Ventura, for Governor Jesse Ventura, the citizens hoping to garner additional publicity for their town. However, the St. Augusta name was reasserted six months later by popular vote.

ST. BONIFACIUS city (Hennepin County) took its name from its Catholic church, consecrated to St. Boniface, the Apostle of the Germans. *Bonifacius* is Latin for "of good fate or fortune."

ST. CHARLES city and township (Winona County) were named for St. Charles of Italy, who was cardinal of Milan and secretary to Pope Pius IV.

ST. CLOUD city (Benton, Sherburne, and Stearns Counties) is the Stearns county seat and was named by John L. Wilson, who chose the name after reading a biography of Napoleon and observing that Empress Josephine spent much of her time at the palace at St. Cloud, near Paris, France. This is the only city in the state that is located in three counties.

ST. CROIX river (Pine, Chisago, and Washington Counties) received its name because a cross had been set at its mouth to mark the grave of a French trader or voyageur. *St. Croix* is French for "Holy Cross."

ST. FRANCIS township (Anoka County) bears the name given in 1680 by Louis Hennepin to what is now the Rum River, commemorating St. Francis of Assisi, founder of the Franciscan order to which Hennepin belonged.

ST. GEORGE township (Benton County) was not named for a saint, but rather for three men named George, who may have been thought saintly by early settlers: George V. Mayhew, George McIntyre, and another George whose last name no one remembers.

ST. HILAIRE city (Pennington County) may have been named for three different people: for a Frenchman named St. Hilaire who lived in a shack near the river and sold gunpowder and tobacco; for a Frenchman named Arthur Yvernault who bought land on which the town site was platted and named it for his hometown in France; or, most likely, for the French statesman and author, Jules Barthélemy-Saint-Hilaire.

ST. JAMES city and township (Watonwan County) origially received a Dakota name suggested by Henry H. Sibley in the company of Elias Drake, president of the St. Paul and Sioux City Railroad. When the pair could not remember the name the following day, Drake proposed that they choose a name they could remember, such as St. James. The city is the county seat.

ST. JOSEPH city and township (Stearns County) bear the name of their church. Another township (Kittson County) was named by Catholic immigrants from Poland for the husband of the Virgin Mary.

ST. LEO city (Yellow Medicine County) was named in honor of the first Pope Leo, also known as Leo the Great, while Leo (Roseau County) was named for Pope Leo XIII.

ST. LOUIS COUNTY is named for the river that flows through it, the largest entering Lake Superior. The river was named by the explorer La Vérendrye, who was honored with the cross of St. Louis, named for the French king Louis IX, who fought in the crusades. St. Louis is the largest county in Minnesota, with an area of 6,611.75 square miles.

ST. LOUIS PARK city (Hennepin County) was developed by the St. Louis Park Improvement Company and its name refers to the Minneapolis and St. Louis Railroad.

ST. MICHAEL city (Wright County) was named for its Catholic church, which was built in 1856.

ST. OLAF township (Otter Tail County) is named for the patron saint of Norway, King Olaf, who is regarded by its people as a champion of national independence.

ST. PAUL city (Ramsey County) is the county seat and capital of Minnesota and was named for a Catholic chapel built in 1841 under the direction of Father Lucian Galtier, who dedicated the church to St. Paul; the settlement, originally called Pig's Eye, soon became known as St. Paul as well.

ST. PAUL PARK city (Washington County) takes part of its name from Charles Parker, one of the city's founders.

ST. PETER city (Nicollet County) is the county seat and was named for the St. Pierre or St. Peter River, as the Minnesota River was called by early French and English

explorers and fur traders, in honor of Pierre Charles
Le Sueur.

ST. WENDEL township (Stearns County) may be named
for the town in Germany, where a chapel remembers
St. Wendelin, patron of herdsmen and farmers. For a
time the town's name was St. Wendell due to a post office error.

SALOL village (Roseau County) takes its name from a
white crystalline powder used as a remedy for rheuma-
tism and neuralgia. Not surprisingly, the name was selected by a druggist, Louis P. Dahlquist, who also served
as superintendent of schools and county treasurer.

SANBORN city (Redwood County) is named in honor of
Sherburn Sanborn, superintendent of the Chicago and
Northwestern Railroad.

SANDSTONE city and township (Pine County) are named
for their extensive quarries of St. Croix sandstone in the
bluffs of the Kettle River.

SANDY township (St. Louis County) is named for its
nearby Sandy and Sand Lakes, which share their names
with over forty bodies of water throughout the state.

SANTIAGO township (Sherburne County) bears the
Spanish name for St. James, shared with the capital of
Chile and a city in Cuba.

SARGEANT city and township (Mower County) were
named in honor of Harry N. Sargeant, a pioneer farmer.

SARTELL city (Benton and Stearns Counties) is named in
honor of first settler Joseph B. Sartell, who operated a
sawmill here.

SAUK CENTRE city and township (Stearns County) received this name because of their central location on the Sauk River between the Sauk Rapids of the Mississippi River and Lake Osakis. The city is the birthplace of Sinclair Lewis and thought to be the fictional Gopher Prairie in his novel *Main Street.*

SAUK RAPIDS township (Benton County) derived this name from the adjoining rapids of the Mississippi River, called Grand Rapids by Zebulon Pike in 1805 and mapped by him as Big Falls. The city (Big Stone County) was originally a trading post for the Winnebago (Ho-Chunk) Indians. The names of the Sauk River (Stearns and Todd Counties) and Le Sauk township (Stearns County) originated from refugee Sauk, or Sac, Indians who came to Osakis Lake from their home in Wisconsin, where they were allied with the Fox Indians.

SAUM village (Beltrami County) is the site of the first consolidated school in Minnesota and the third in the United States. The origin of the name is unknown.

SAVAGE city (Scott County) was named in honor of Marion W. Savage, who ran a horse-training farm here and owned the famous champion trotting horse, Dan Patch. *See also* Lake Marion

SAVANNA lake (Aitkin County) and the West and East Savanna Rivers were named in reference to nearby savannas, more commonly called prairies.

SAWTOOTH mountains (Cook County) are named for the saw-like profile of their serrate hills and low mountains.

SCANDIA township (Washington County) is the site where the first Swedish immigrant to Minnesota settled, named in reference to the Scandinavian peninsula. Similarly, Scandia Grove village (Nicollet County) is one of the oldest Swedish settlements in Minnesota. Its first settlers were Norwegians, but the community developed with the arrival of a small Swedish Lutheran congregation.

SCANLON city (Carlton County) was named for M. Joseph Scanlon, a logging and lumber entrepreneur.

SCHLEY railroad station (Cass County) was named for Adm. Winfield S. Schley, who commanded the "Flying Squadron" during the Spanish-American War.

SCHOOLCRAFT township (Hubbard County) was named for its river, which Henry R. Schoolcraft canoed in 1832 while searching for the headwaters of the Mississippi River. He was an explorer, Indian agent, mapmaker, and the author of six volumes on U.S. Indians.

SCOTT COUNTY was named in honor of Gen. Winfield Scott, who was commander in chief of the U.S. Army from 1841 to 1861.

SEAFORTH city (Redwood County) received its name from Loch Seaforth, an arm of the sea in the Hebrides, Scotland.

SEBEKA city (Wadena County) takes its name from the Ojibwe language, meaning "the village or town beside the river," in this case, the Redeye River.

SEVEN BEAVER lake (St. Louis County) is the principal head of the St. Louis River and was named by the Ojibwe for beavers shot or trapped here.

SHAKOPEE city (Scott County) is the county seat and was named for the leader of a Dakota band living here. The hereditary name of successive leaders, *Shakopee* means "six."

SHAMROCK township (Aitkin County) was named by Irish settlers for the plant that is the national emblem of Ireland.

SHELDON township (Houston County) took its name from Julius C. Sheldon, a Connecticut native and township proprietor who stayed only long enough to leave his name.

SHELL RIVER township and **SHELL CITY** village (Wadena County) get their names from the mussel or clam shells of the Shell River.

SHERBURN city (Martin County) is possibly named for Sherburne S. Merrill, a Southern Minnesota Railroad official, or for the wife of an officer of the Chicago, Milwaukee and St. Paul Railroad.

SHERBURNE COUNTY was named in honor of Moses Sherburne, who was an associate justice of Minnesota Territory's supreme court from 1853 to 1857.

SHETEK township and lake (Murray County) take the Ojibwe word for pelican.

SHEVLIN city and township (Clearwater County) were named in honor of Thomas H. Shevlin, president of several logging and lumber companies.

SHIELDSVILLE township (Rice County) was named in honor of Gen. James Shields, who encouraged many

Irish colonists to establish homestead farms in this township.

SHINGLE creek (Hennepin County) joins the Mississippi River in north Minneapolis and probably takes its name from the shingle mill that was located at its mouth in 1852.

SHINGOBEE township (Cass County) received this name from its creek, which has the general Ojibwe word for the spruce, balsam fir, and arbor vitae species of evergreens common to the region.

SHOREVIEW city (Ramsey County) is named for its many lakes and their accompanying views.

SHOREWOOD city (Hennepin County) was named for its location on Lake Minnetonka and for its wooded home sites, which were developed into a residential community.

SIBILANT lake (Clearwater County) is named for its form resembling the letter S.

SIBLEY COUNTY and townships (Crow Wing and Sibley Counties) were named in honor of Gen. Henry H. Sibley, pioneer, governor, and military defender of Minnesota.

SIGEL township (Brown County) and lake (Lyon County) commemorate Franz Sigel, a Civil War general who visited New Ulm and this township in 1873.

SILVER BAY city (Lake County) may have been named for many reasons, but the most common story is that in 1903 the captain of the *America* needed a name for a shipping point at the site and suggested the name for the bay. The city then took its name from the bay.

SILVER CREEK township (Wright County) was named for the creek that flows through it, though we're not sure how the creek earned its name.

SILVER LAKE city (McLeod County) and township (Martin County) are named for their locations near Silver Lake and the South and North Silver Lakes, respectively.

SILVERTON township (Pennington County) was probably named for the silverberry, a shrub with whitish leaves and edible berries of a silvery color, common along the Red River Valley.

SISEEBAKWET lake (Itasca County) has an Ojibwe name meaning "Sugar Lake," referring to production of maple sugar here.

SLAYTON city and township (Murray County) are named in honor of Charles W. Slayton, the founder and chief proprietor of the township and an agent who brought English colonists to the area. The city is the county seat.

SLEEPY EYE city (Brown County) was named, like its adjoining lake, for a leader of the Sisseton Dakota. His name referred to a facial characteristic: his eyes were usually only about half open.

SMOKY HOLLOW township (Cass County) was named by an early settler in remembrance of his former home in New York State or possibly for Washington Irving's *The Legend of Sleepy Hollow.*

SNELLING fort (Hennepin County) commemorates Col. Josiah Snelling, commander at Fort St. Anthony beginning in 1820. He erected its permanent buildings, and the fort was subsequently renamed in his honor.

SNOWBALL village (Itasca County) is no more, having been destroyed by fire. Its demise calls to mind the phrase "a snowball's chance in hell."

SOBIESKI city (Morrison County) was named for Prince Sobieski, hero of Poland.

SOLANA village (Aitkin County) was named by a surveyor from Salinas, Kans., who changed the spelling, or possibly for a lumber camp cook who did everything slowly, that is "slow" Anna.

SOMERSET township (Steele County) is said to have received its name after the postmaster's tent was turned over by high wind, causing it to somersault. A change of spelling brought about Somerset.

SOUDAN village and mine (St. Louis County) were named by D. H. Bacon, who, chilled by the severity of local winters, thought of the contrasting tropical climate of Africa's Sudan region.

SOUTH BEND township (Blue Earth County) derived its name from the fact that the Minnesota River makes its great southern bend on the township's northern boundary.

SOUTH ST. PAUL city (Dakota County) is possibly named because of its location in regard to St. Paul.

SPARTA township (Chippewa County) was named for Sparta, Wis., where a number of settlers had previously lived. It in turn was named for an ancient Greek city.

SPECTACLE lake (Isanti County) is named for its shape, similar to a pair of eyeglasses.

SPICER city (Kandiyohi County) was named in honor of John M. Spicer, founder and owner of the town site.

SPLITROCK village (Lake County) was a small settlement and logging camp on the Split Rock River, which was named for a rock gorge near its mouth.

SPOONER township (Lake of the Woods County) was named in honor of Judge Marshall A. Spooner of Bemidji, who helped obtain incorporation papers for the township in 1905.

SPRING LAKE township (Scott County) was named for its northern lake, which has a large spring running from it.

SPRING LAKE PARK city (Anoka and Ramsey Counties) is a residential community that was named by a real estate agent of Bronson-Erickson who, as the story goes, mistakenly thought that a broken water main in Wood Lake was an underground freshwater spring. More likely, the developer chose the name because it was pleasant to the ear and descriptive of the area.

SPRING VALLEY city and township (Fillmore County) were named for several nearby large springs, one of which supplied the early waterworks.

SPRINGFIELD city (Brown County) may bear the name of Springfield, Mass., but its residents trace its origin to a large spring on the north side of the Cottonwood River.

STANCHFIELD township (Isanti County) as well as the Lower Stanchfield Brook, Lower Stanchfield Lake, Stanchfield Creek, and two Upper Stanchfield Lakes are named in honor of Daniel Stanchfield, who was the first to explore the extensive pineries of the Rum River.

STANTON township (Goodhue County) honors William Stanton, an early settler noted for his hospitality. He was known to have accommodated as many as fifty travelers in the same night.

STAPLES city and township (Todd County) commemorate the Stillwater lumber family who had logging and manufacturing interests here.

STAR township (Pennington County) was named after residents heard "Zenith" proposed and chose instead the current name, deeming Zenith too difficult to pronounce. The name refers to Polaris or the North Star.

STARBUCK city (Pope County) has four versions of its naming: 1) for the oxen Star and Buck, who hauled materials for an early bridge; 2) for Sidney Starbuck, a director of the Little Falls and Dakota Railroad; 3) for W. H. Starbuck, a builder of railroads; or 4) for an early settler whose last name was Sagbaken, which was transformed into Starbuck.

STARK village (Chisago County) was named in honor of Lars J. Stark, who was the first postmaster here.

STAVANGER post office (Yellow Medicine County) is named for the fjord, city, and district of this name in southern Norway.

STEAMBOAT river and lake (Hubbard County) were named because of their location on a steamboat route from Leech Lake.

STEARNS COUNTY mistakenly commemorates Charles T. Stearns, member of the council of the territorial legislature in 1854 and 1855. The county was to have honored Isaac I. Stevens, territorial governor of Washington, but at its registration a bureaucrat changed the name to Stearns. When the error was discovered, the county residents decided not to protest, maintaining that Stearns was also an honorable man. Stevens would be recognized in the name of another county.

STEELE COUNTY is named in honor of a prominent pioneer of Minneapolis, Franklin Steele, who was active in improving waterpower on the Mississippi River and building the cities of St. Anthony and Minneapolis.

STEEN city (Rock County) was named in honor of brothers John and Ole Steen, Norwegian immigrants who homesteaded this site.

STEPHEN city (Marshall County) was named in honor of George Stephen, an associate of railroad magnate James J. Hill and president of the Canadian Pacific Railway, later titled Baron Mount Stephen for a Rocky Mountain peak named for him.

STEVENS COUNTY and township were named in honor of Isaac I. Stevens, who in 1853 commanded the expedition making the northern surveys for a railroad to the Pacific Ocean.

STEWARTVILLE township (Olmsted County) was founded by Charles Stewart and named in his honor.

STILLWATER city (Washington County) is the county seat, and its name was suggested by the stillness of the water and in connection to a settler's hometown in Maine. Stillwater is the oldest county seat in Minnesota.

STRAND township (Norman County) was named by Norwegian settlers because its poplar groves bordering the beaches of the glacial Lake Agassiz, seen at a long distance from the vast prairie of the Red River Valley, resembled an ocean strand or shore.

STRATHCONA city (Roseau County) commemorates Donald A. Smith, later Lord Strathcona, Canadian railroad executive and friend of James J. Hill.

STRINGTOWN village (Fillmore County) earned its name because all the settlers built their houses in a ravine along the road, thus stringing out the village for some distance. It was earlier called String Out Town and later renamed Amherst.

STROUT village (Meeker County) was named for Capt. Richard Strout, leader of an army company in the Acton area during the Dakota War.

STUNTZ township (St. Louis County) was named for George Stuntz, who made extensive surveys in northern Wisconsin and Minnesota, including one on the Mesabi Range, and was an early settler of the Duluth-Superior region.

STURGEON LAKE city and township (Pine County) were named for the large lake to their east. Sturgeon River township (Koochiching County) is likewise named for its river, which was probably a translation from the Ojibwe for the ascent of lake or rock sturgeon to this stream.

SUGAR BUSH township (Beltrami County) was named for its maple trees, used by both Indians and settlers for making sugar.

SUMMERVILLE township (Koochiching County) was named for Margaret Sommers, a widow and the only woman residing in the original township in 1905.

SUMNER township (Fillmore County) honors Massachusetts senator Charles Sumner, an uncompromising opponent of slavery.

SUMTER township (McLeod County) was named for Fort Sumter near Charleston, S.C., site of the first battle of the Civil War.

SUNRISE township (Chisago County) received its name from the lake and river whose Ojibwe name is translated as "Sun-keep-rising."

SUOMI village (Itasca County) was named by its first settlers for their native country, using a traditional name for Finland.

SUPERIOR lake (St. Louis, Lake, and Cook Counties) is the largest freshwater lake in the world and was named *Grand Lac* on a 1632 map by Samuel de Champlain, which became Lake Superior on Father Jacques Marquette's 1673 map. The Ojibwe name for it means "Great Water." The lake runs 150 miles along Minnesota's northeast border.

SVEA village (Kandiyohi County) has the name used by a local Swedish Lutheran congregation, the feminine word for Sweden. A township (Kittson County) also shares this name.

SVEADAHL village (Watonwan County) was originally settled by Swedish immigrants, and its name means "Sweden valley or dale."

SWANBURG village (Crow Wing County) was named for a Swede, Swan P. Hanson, who acquired land in the early 1900s to create a railroad community. The railroad passed by and Norwegians settled the area instead.

Though the village was named for him, Hanson never lived here.

SWEET township (Pipestone County) was named in honor of the county's first settler, Daniel E. Sweet, who platted the city of Pipestone.

SWENODA township (Swift County) and lake (Pope County) have a composite name complimenting Swedish, Norwegian, and Danish settlers.

SWIFT COUNTY was named in honor of Henry A. Swift, governor of Minnesota in 1863.

SYLVAN township (Cass County) is named for its lake, referring to the woods or groves on its shores. The Ojibwe name for this lake means "fish trap lake."

SYNNES township (Stevens County) suggests no broken commandments but was instead named for an early settler.

T

TACONITE city (Itasca County) was laid out by the Oliver Mining Company, which had opened the Holman Mine here. Taconite is a rock that is mined for its low-grade iron ore.

TAMARACK city (Aitkin County) grew up out of the extensive peat- and tamarack-covered bogs when the Northern Pacific laid track from Duluth to Brainerd.

TAOPI city (Mower County) was named in honor of a leader of a farmer band of the Dakota whose name means "Wounded Man." He was one of the first converts to Christianity at the Redwood mission on the Minnesota River.

TARA township (Swift and Traverse Counties) was named for the hill of Tara near Dublin, Ireland.

TARGET lake (Houston County) is named for rifle practice that used to take place here.

TAYLORS FALLS city (Chisago County) was named for a pioneer, Jesse Taylor, and for Joshua Taylor, to whom the former sold his claim in 1846.

TEGNER township (Kittson County) was named for an important nineteenth-century Swedish poet, Esaias Tegner.

TENHASSEN township (Martin County) has a Dakota name in changed form. If spelled correctly, it would share its name with another township, named in reference to sugar maple trees. *See* Chanhassen

TENSTRIKE city (Beltrami County) may have taken its name from a bowling term for when the first ball knocks down all ten pins or from the remark of a prosperous local trader who exclaimed, "I sure made a tenstrike here."

TEPEEOTA village (Wabasha County) was founded in 1856 on an island of the Mississippi River but abandoned during the financial panic of 1857. Its Dakota name means "many houses," but, alas, there are none left.

TERREBONNE township (Red Lake County) has a French name meaning "good land," also the name of a county in Quebec.

THIEF RIVER FALLS city (Pennington County) and the Thief River are somewhat misnamed. After a small encampment of Dakota were destroyed by invading Ojibwe, the Ojibwe called the river Secret Earth River, for the earthen embankment erected by the Dakota as a protective barrier against attack. Through erroneous pronunciation of the name and misunderstanding of its intended significance, the early fur traders changed it to Stealing Earth River and thence to Thief River. The city is the county seat.

THOMSON township (Carlton County) was named by officers of the St. Paul and Duluth Railroad in honor of David Thompson, a Canadian explorer, but it has generally been spelled as if for James Thomson, a Scottish poet, while still others believe it was named for J. Edgar Thompson, president of the Pennsylvania Central Railroad.

TINTAH city and township (Traverse County) received their name from a Dakota word meaning "a prairie."

TOAD LAKE township (Becker County) received its name from its large lake and the outflowing Toad River. The name is a translation from the Ojibwe.

TODD COUNTY was named for John Blair Smith Todd, commander of Fort Ripley.

TOFTE city and township (Cook County) were named for early settlers with this surname, derived from their former home in the district of Bergen, Norway.

TOGO post office (Itasca County) may have a name that refers to its popularity as a destination, but it was actually named for Adm. Togo of the Japanese navy, which sank the Russian fleet during the Russo-Japanese War in 1905.

TOPELIUS village (Otter Tail County) was named for Zachris Topelius, a distinguished Swedish educator, historian, poet, and novelist of Helsingfors, Finland. For a time, the name was misspelled by the railroad and the post office as Dopelius.

TOQUA township (Big Stone County) received its name from the two Tokua Lakes in Graceville and a similar pair of lakes in this township, referring to a Dakota band having a moose as a totem: *ta* for moose and *kara* for the Kahra band.

TOWER city (St. Louis County) was named in honor of Charlemagne Tower, a Philadelphia attorney who was connected with the Minnesota Iron Company and the Duluth and Iron Range Railroad Company.

TRACY city (Lyon County) was named in honor of John F. Tracy, a former president of the Chicago and Northwestern Railroad.

TRANSIT township (Sibley County) is uniquely named for the instrument used in railway surveys.

TRAVERSE township (Nicollet County) was commonly called "Traverse des Sioux" or "Crossing of the Sioux" because the Minnesota River was crossed here on a much-used trail from St. Paul and Fort Snelling to the upper Minnesota valley and the Red River Valley.

TRAVERSE COUNTY received its name from the lake, from the French *Lac Travers,* a translation of the Dakota name, which means "lake lying crosswise."

TRELIPE township (Cass County) and **TULABY** lake (Becker and Mahnomen Counties) are named, with various spellings, for the tullibee, a fish commonly found in the lakes of northern Minnesota.

TRIMONT city (Martin County) was named as a result of a merger between the towns of Triumph and Monterey, the former named for the Triumph Creamery Company.

TROY township (Pipestone County) received its name from Troy, N.Y., by vote of the settlers after numerous names had been proposed and rejected. Daniel Whigam, at whose home the township meeting was held, suggested Troy, the place of manufacture stamped on his kitchen stove. Another township (Renville County) is likewise named for the ancient city in Asia Minor, scene of the Trojan War.

TRUMAN city (Martin County) is named for Truman Clark, son of J. T. Clark, a vice president of the Chicago,

St. Paul, Minneapolis and Omaha Railroad. As an added incentive for adopting the name, several families named True lived in this region.

TUMULI township (Otter Tail County) has a Latin name meaning "burial mounds," probably referring to the drift hills in the eastern section of the township.

TURTLE LAKE township (Beltrami County) bears the name of its large lake, a translation from the Ojibwe, as does the Turtle River, which flows from it. Another township (Cass County) is similarly named for its Turtle Lakes.

TWEET post office (Pennington County) was named not for a local aviary but for an early Norwegian settler, Jacob Tweet.

TWO HARBORS city and township (Lake County) are named for their location on two natural harbors, Agate and Burlington Bays on Lake Superior. The city is the county seat.

TYRO township (Yellow Medicine County) bears a name meaning "a beginner." Organized in 1879, it can no longer be considered one, however.

UDOLPHO township (Mower County) was named by one of its pioneers for the book by Mrs. Ann Ward Radcliffe, *The Mysteries of Udolpho*, a highly fanciful romance set in seventeenth-century Italy.

UNION GROVE township (Meeker County) received its name from the grove where a union church had been built.

UPSALA city (Morrison County) was named by Swedish settlers for the city of Uppsala in Sweden.

VADNAIS HEIGHTS city (Ramsey County) was named for Lake Vadnais, which honors Jean Vadnais, an early settler.

VALLERS township (Lyon County) was named by Norwegian pioneer Ole O. Brenna. Poor Ole! He wanted to name the town *Valla*, a Norwegian word meaning "valley." But because the handwriting on the application was illegible, county commissioners made the name Vallers instead.

VASA township (Goodhue County) was named in honor of Gustavus Vasa, king of Sweden, better known as Gustavus I, the founder of the Lutheran Church.

VEGA township (Marshall County) bears the name of the ship in which Swedish explorer Baron Nordenskjöld in 1878–79 traversed the Arctic Ocean, passed through the Bering Strait, and returned home via the Suez Canal.

VELDT township (Marshall County) was initially called Roosevelt for President Theodore Roosevelt. Because that name was already in use, it was changed to this Dutch word, used in South Africa, meaning "a prairie or a thinly wooded tract." Note that the township nearly retains the final syllable of its original name.

VENOAH lake (Carlton County) is named with the nicknames of Judge F. A. Watkins's daughters, Winona and Marie.

VERDI township (Lincoln County) was named for the Italian composer Giuseppe Verdi. The name means "verdant or verdure," apt descriptions of the lush prairie township.

VERGAS city (Otter Tail County) takes the name from one of four in the "V" series used to designate Soo Line sleeping cars that traveled between Minneapolis and Winnipeg. The others were Viking, Venlo, and Venus.

VERMILION iron range (Cook, Itasca, and Lake Counties) was named, with altered spelling, for the Vermillion Lake and River in St. Louis County, as was Vermillion township (Dakota County). A translation of the Ojibwe name, it refers to the red and golden sunset reflection on the smooth lake surface.

VERNDALE city (Wadena County) was named in honor of Helen Vernette "Vernie" Smith, a granddaughter of one of its pioneer settlers.

VERNON CENTER city and township (Blue Earth County) received their name from the original platters of the area, who came from Mount Vernon, Ohio. Numerous places with this name commemorate the eighteenth-century British admiral Edward Vernon, including Vernon township (Dodge County).

VERONA township (Faribault County) takes its name from the northern Italian province and its chief city, from which comes the title of Shakespeare's *Two Gentlemen of Verona*.

VESELI village (Rice County) was named for a city in southern Bohemia (now the Czech Republic) and means "hilarity, happiness, contentment, cheerfulness."

VICTORIA city (Carver County) was named for the queen of England, though it is unknown who decided to honor her.

VIKING township (Marshall County) was named with a Scandinavian word, often translated as "sea king," that more correctly denoted any member of the early medieval pirate crews of Northmen who ravaged the coasts of western and southern Europe.

VILLARD city (Pope County) and township (Todd County) were named in honor of Henry Villard, president of the Northern Pacific Railroad Company from 1881 to 1883, when its transcontinental line was completed.

VINELAND township (Polk County) and village and port of Mille Lacs (Mille Lacs County) were named for the early Norse settlement on the northeast coast of North America, in the Icelandic language *Vinland*, meaning "wineland," for the grapes found there.

VIOLA township (Olmsted County) was named at the suggestion of Irwin N. Wetmore for the village near La Crosse, Wis.

VIRGINIA city (St. Louis County) was named for the virgin region and also for the home state of a mine proprietor.

VISTA village (Waseca County) was named by Swedish settlers for a district in Sweden.

VOYAGEURS national park (St. Louis County) was named for the canoeists of the fur trade and contains fifty-five miles of the old fur-trade route between the Great Lakes and the continent's interior. It is the only national park without a road.

WABANICA township (Lake of the Woods County) received its name from *waban*, the Ojibwe word for east and also for the twilight, or dawn, of the morning.

WABASHA COUNTY and city, which is the county seat, commemorate a line of Dakota leaders who for three successive generations exerted great influence over their people. Originally spelled *Wapashaw*, the word means "red leaf."

WABASSO city (Redwood County) takes its name from Henry W. Longfellow's *The Song of Hiawatha,* for the Ojibwe word for rabbit.

WABEDO township (Cass County) received its name from the lake, which was named by the Ojibwe after a party of Dakota killed an Ojibwe hunter named *Wab-ud-ow,* or "White Gore."

WACONIA city and township (Carver County) bear the Dakota name of their large lake, meaning "fountain or spring."

WACOUTA township (Goodhue County) is named for a leader of the Mdewakanton band of Dakota. His name means "the shooter."

WADENA COUNTY and city and township take their name from an archaic Ojibwe word signifying "a little round hill." Wadena is also a personal name among the Ojibwe. The city is the county seat.

WAHKON city, island, and bay (Mille Lacs County) use the Dakota name of Mille Lacs, spelled *mde*, water, and *wakan*, meaning "spiritual, sacred, consecrated, wonderful, incomprehensible."

WAITE PARK city (Stearns County) was named for Henry C. Waite of nearby St. Cloud, who was a lawyer and merchant and member of the state constitutional convention, legislature, and senate.

WAKEFIELD township (Stearns County) was named for Samuel Wakefield, chairman of its first board of supervisors.

WAKEMUP village (St. Louis County) has nothing whatever to do with rousing indolent settlers with reveille. Instead this is the anglicized name of an Ojibwe leader, *Way-ko-mah-wub,* who lived on a western bay on Vermillion Lake.

WALBO village (Isanti County) was founded by Swedes, in whose language *wal* is a type of fish.

WALDEN townships (Cass and Pope Counties) bear the name of a pond near Concord, Mass., beside which Henry D. Thoreau built a hut and lived from 1845 to 1847, as recounted in his book *Walden, or Life in the Woods.*

WALHALLA township (Lake of the Woods County) is named from Norse mythology for the hall of Odin, also spelled *Valhalla,* the afterworld for the souls of warriors slain in battle.

WALKER city (Cass County) is the county seat and was named in honor of Thomas B. Walker, who had large lumbering and land interests in Cass County and elsewhere in the state.

WALNUT GROVE city (Redwood County) was named for a grove of black walnut trees. Charles Ingalls, father of Laura Ingalls Wilder, was the first justice of this community.

WANAMINGO city and township (Goodhue County) were almost wholly settled by Norwegians who for unknown reasons gave the town the Indian name of a heroine of a popular novel.

WANDA city (Redwood County) is named from the Ojibwe word *wanenda*, meaning "to forget" or "forgetfulness," although we have made certain to remember it here.

WARBA city (Itasca County) was named by A. A. Hall, who won a contest to determine the city's name. He selected the Ojibwe word *warbasibi*, which has been variously interpreted as "resting place" or "white swan." The spelling was later converted to Warba.

WARMAN village and creek (Kanabec County) were named in honor of S. M. Warman, a quarry owner who was killed by a falling derrick. In a curious juxtaposition, the village is located in Peace Township.

WARREN city (Marshall County) is the county seat and was named in honor of Charles H. Warren, general passenger agent of the St. Paul, Minneapolis and Manitoba Railroad, later the Great Northern Railway. The former river is named for Gen. Gouverneur K. Warren, who explored the region in 1868. Flowing from the glacial Lake Agassiz, the river formed Big Stone Lake and Lake Traverse, and a portion of the ancient river course between the lakes, a distance of nearly five miles, is known as Browns Valley.

WARROAD township (Roseau County) is situated on the mouth of the river from which it takes its name. The river was in a neutral tract between the warring Ojibwe and Dakota, and, as a thoroughfare for these hostile groups, it was known as a "road of war."

WASECA COUNTY and city, the county seat, are named with the Dakota word meaning "rich, especially in provisions."

WASHINGTON COUNTY and the township and lake (Le Sueur County) were named for George Washington, the father of our country.

WASIOJA township (Dodge County) bears a Dakota name meaning "Pine River," referring to the Zumbro River.

WATAB township (Benton County) is named for the river with the Ojibwe word for the long and very slender roots of both the tamarack and jack pine, which the Indians dug, split, and used as threads in sewing birchbark canoes.

WATERLYNN village (Waseca County) has a poetic name, probably taken from the surnames of Mr. Waters and Mr. Chamberlain, who vainly tried to develop this village on the Le Sueur River.

WATERTOWN city and township (Carver County) received this name for their plentiful supply of water in the form of several lakes and a branch of the Crow River. Many of the city's early industries benefited from the river's waterpower. Similarly, another township (Crow

Wing County) was named for its lakes and the Pine River.

WATERVILLE city and township (Le Sueur County) have this name in reference to the adjoining Lakes Tetonka and Sakatah, through which the Cannon River flows, and to White Water Creek, tributary to Lake Sakatah.

WATKINS city (Meeker County) was named for an official of the Minneapolis and Pacific Railroad. It is the hometown of U.S. senator and presidential candidate Eugene McCarthy.

WATONWAN COUNTY was named for the river, which was thought to use a Dakota word for "I see" but which may have been misspelled from *watanwan*, meaning "fish bait."

WAUBUN city (Mahnomen County) has an Ojibwe name meaning "the east," "the morning," and "the twilight of dawn."

WAUKON township (Norman County) has a Dakota name meaning "spiritual, sacred, wonderful," probably in reference to the grand view westward over the Red River Valley.

WAVERLY city (Wright County) takes its name from the adjacent Big and Little Waverly Lakes, which were named for a town in New York State, which was in turn named for Sir Walter Scott's Waverly novels. It was the home of U.S. senator and vice president Hubert H. Humphrey.

WAWINA township (Itasca County) received this name from the Ojibwe, meaning "I mention him frequently."

WAYZATA city (Hennepin County) was named with a slight altering of *Waziyata*, a Dakota word meaning "at the pines, the north." The town, on the north side of Lake Minnetonka, actually had very few pines.

WEIMER township (Jackson County) was named by Charles Winzer, the first settler, in honor of his former home in Saxe-Weimar, Germany, but the name was recorded with this misspelling.

WELCH township (Goodhue County) commemorates Abraham E. Welch, who served in the First and Fourth Minnesota Regiments during the Civil War and died from wounds received at the battle of Vicksburg.

WELCOME city (Martin County) was named in honor of Alfred M. Welcome, who farmed at its southwest side. The name presumably also indicates how visitors feel upon their arrival.

WELLS city (Faribault County) receives the maiden surname of Mrs. Clark W. Thompson. The town is in Clark Township, which was named for her husband. The town is also known for its numerous flowing wells, which were undeveloped at the time the town was named, suggesting that a name can equal destiny.

WELLS township and lake (Rice County) and creek (Goodhue County) commemorate James Wells, often called "Bully" Wells, who operated a fur trading post on Lake Pepin. He was mysteriously murdered in 1863, ten years after establishing a post on Wells Lake.

WESCOTT railroad station (Dakota County) was named for a prominent pioneer, James Wescott, who served in the First Minnesota Heavy Artillery in the Civil War and was county treasurer from 1860 to 1862.

WEST NEWTON township (Nicollet County) was named partly to honor James Newton, an early settler and Civil War veteran, but principally to commemorate the *West Newton,* the first steamer to ascend the Minnesota River any distance above the mouth of the Blue Earth River.

WEST ST. PAUL city (Dakota County) was incorporated in 1889. An earlier city by the same name was originally incorporated in Dakota County in 1858 but was annexed by Ramsey County in 1874, becoming a ward of the city of St. Paul. The name was subsequently changed to Riverview in 1918, after 3,434 citizens petitioned for the change, while only fifty preferred that the new name be South Side.

WESTERN and **EASTERN** townships (Otter Tail County) are named in relation to each other: the former is the most southwestern township in the county, while the latter is the most southeastern.

WHEATON city (Traverse County) is the county seat and is named in honor of Daniel T. Wheaton of Morris, a surveyor for the Fargo and Southern Railroad. He advised that this new village be named Swedenburg for the Swedish owners of the site, but residents preferred to name it for him.

WHISKEY creek (Wilkin County) was named for unlawful sales of whiskey to soldiers from Fort Abercrombie who visited dugout huts located beside this stream.

WHITE BEAR LAKE city and **WHITE BEAR** township (Ramsey County) receive the name of the large White Bear Lake, from an old Indian legend about a bear whose spirit is said to haunt the island and lake. Another township (Pope County) was named for an Ojibwe leader whose grave was on the south side of Lake Minnewaska.

WHITE EARTH township (Becker County) is named for the village of White Earth, the location of the U.S. government agency of the White Earth Reservation, from the Ojibwe name for the lake, translated as "the-place-of-white-clay-lake."

WHITED township (Kanabec County) was named for Oric O. Whited, who was superintendent of schools in Olmsted County, practiced law in Minneapolis, and owned land in Kanabec County.

WILDER city and township (Jackson County) honor Amherst H. Wilder, a St. Paul businessman and railroad builder.

WILKIN COUNTY commemorates Col. Alexander Wilkin of the Ninth Minnesota Regiment, who was killed in the Civil War battle at Tupelo, Miss., on July 14, 1864.

WILLBORG village (Clearwater County) was named for Martin Willborg, its first postmaster.

WILLERNIE city (Washington County) has a name meaning "wildwood." It is located next to Wildwood Amusement Park.

WILLIAMS city (Lake of the Woods County) was named for two Williams—William Mason and George Williams—who staked claims at this site in 1901. The township (Koochiching County) honors James Williams, who operated a portable sawmill here.

WILLMAR city, township, and lake (Kandiyohi County) were named for Leon Willmar of Belgium, who was the agent for the European bondholders of the St. Paul and Pacific Railroad Company and owner of several hundred acres in the county. The city is the county seat.

WILLMONT township (Nobles County) received this name as the result of a compromise between two factions in the community: one wanted the township named Willumet, the other Lamont. The nearby city further altered the name, to Wilmont.

WILNO village (Lincoln County) was settled primarily by Polish immigrants, who named most of the streets for Polish cities or heroes. The village was named for the second city, Vilnius or Wilnius, of old Poland, now the capital of Lithuania.

WINDEMERE township (Pine County) received its name with altered spelling from Lake Windermere, the largest lake in England. The name was suggested by an early homesteader, William Pitt, who was born and raised on the shores of that lake.

WINDOM city and township (Cottonwood County) honor William Windom, who served terms in Congress and the U.S. Senate and was secretary of the treasury under President William Henry Harrison. The city is the county seat.

WINNEBAGO city (Faribault County) and townships (Faribault and Houston Counties) are named for the Winnebago (Ho-Chunk) Indians, who lived on Long Prairie Reservation from 1855 to 1863.

WINNESHIEK prairie (Wright County) was named in honor of the Winnebago (Ho-Chunk) leader who with his tribe spent several years on Long Prairie Reservation and in Blue Earth County.

WINNIBIGOSHISH lake (Cass County) has an Ojibwe name that Joseph Nicollet translates as "miserable-wretched-dirty-water," because the lake is relatively shallow and large waves stir up its mud and sand bottom.

WINONA COUNTY and lake and city, the county seat, were named for a Dakota woman, cousin of the last leader named Wabasha. Winona is often the name given by the Dakota to a first-born female child.

WINSTED city, township, and lake (McLeod County) received their name from the village founder, Eli F. Lewis, who was from Winsted, Conn.

WINTER ROAD river (Lake of the Woods County) was the starting point for a dog sled trail or "winter road" that left the Rainy River and ran about fifty miles to the north shore of Red Lake.

WINTHROP city (Sibley County) received its name from the officers of the Minneapolis and St. Louis Railroad. Who Winthrop was, however, remains a mystery.

WITOKA village (Winona County) was named for the daughter of the war chief of Wabasha's band, who was rescued from the Sauk (Sac) Indians by her father here.

WOLVERTON city and township (Wilkin County) were named in honor of Dr. William D. Wolverton, a physician at Fort Abercrombie, across the Red River in North Dakota, who owned land in this township.

WOODBURY city and township (Washington County) were named in honor of Judge Levi Woodbury, a special friend of the chairman of the board of county commissioners. Woodbury was governor of New Hampshire and a U.S. cabinet officer, U.S. senator, and Supreme Court justice.

WOODROW township (Cass County) was named for President Woodrow Wilson.

WOODVILLE township (Waseca County) honors brothers Eri and Loren M. Wood, who were among its first settlers.

WORM lake (Grant County) is named for its irregular and worm-like form.

WORTHINGTON city and township (Nobles County) were named for the mother of Mary D. Miller, whose maiden name was Worthington. Her husband, Dr. A. P. Miller, was a town founder and newspaper editor. The city is the county seat.

WRENSHALL city and township (Carlton County) were named for C. C. Wrenshall, who was in charge of bridge maintenance and repair for the Northern Pacific Railroad.

WRIGHT COUNTY was named in honor of New York statesman Silas Wright, a congressman, U.S. senator, and governor of New York. The township (Carlton County) honors George B. Wright, a railroad man who founded Fergus Falls, and Charles B. Wright, director of the Northern Pacific Railroad.

WYANDOTTE township (Pennington County) bears the aboriginal name of a confederation of four Iroquoian tribes, called *Huron* by the French.

WYANETT township (Isanti County) was named for a village in northern Illinois using an Indian word meaning "beautiful."

WYLIE township (Red Lake County) was named for William Wylie, an early farmer who also served as a schoolteacher.

WYOMING city and township (Chisago County) derive their names from the Wyoming Valley in Luzerne County, Pa., the former home of settlers. The name is from the Delaware Indians and means "large plains" or "extensive meadows."

YELLOW BANK township (Lac qui Parle County) received the name of the river, referring to the yellowish glacial drift seen in its eroded bluffs.

YELLOW MEDICINE COUNTY and city are named for the river, translated from the Dakota word for the root of the moonseed, which grows in this region.

YOUNG AMERICA city, township, and a small lake (Carver County) are named with an expression of the vigor and progressiveness of the young people of the United States.

YUCATAN township (Houston County) was first called Utica, but to avoid confusion with other places of that name it was changed to its present and similar-sounding name, for the large peninsula in Mexico.

Z

ZIMMERMAN city (Sherburne County) was named for Henry Zimmerman, its first postmaster.

ZIPPEL township, creek, and bay (Lake of the Woods County) were named for William M. Zippel, who was for many years a fisherman on Lake of the Woods.

ZUMBRO township and **ZUMBRO FALLS** city (Wabasha County) and **ZUMBROTA** city and township (Goodhue County) are named for the Zumbro River, the spelling and pronunciation much changed from the original French, *Rivière des Embarras*, or "the river of difficulties or encumbrances," so called because of driftwood that made canoe navigation a challenge. *See* Embarrass

APPENDIX
Names Arranged by County

AITKIN
Arthyde
Ball Bluff
Blind
Cornish
Esquagamah
Farm Island
Glory
Horseshoe
Idun
Logan
McGregor
Palisade
Quadna
Redtop
Savanna
Shamrock
Solana
Tamarack

ANOKA
Andover
Bethel
Blaine
Burns
Centerville

Circle Pines
Columbia
   Heights
Columbus
Coon Rapids
Fridley
Grow
Ham Lake
Lexington
Lino Lakes
Linwood
Nowthen
Oak Grove
Ramsey
Rum
St. Francis
Spring Lake
   Park

BECKER
Audubon
Cuba
Detroit Lakes
Frazee
Height of Land
Ice Cracking

Many Point
Ogema
Osage
Runeberg
Toad Lake
Tulaby
   (see Trelipe)
White Earth

BELTRAMI
Battle
Bemidji
Birch Island
Black Duck
Blackduck
Buzzle
Cormant
Debs
Funkley
Moose Lake
Nebish
North Pole
Northern
Ponemah
Puposky
Quiring

Roosevelt
Saum
Sugar Bush
Tenstrike
Turtle Lake

BENTON
Foley
Glendorado
Halfway
Mayhew Lake
Peace Rock
St. Cloud
St. George
Sartell
Sauk Rapids
Watab

BIG STONE
Artichoke
Beardsley
Browns Valley
Graceville
Moonshine
Odessa
Ortonville
Sauk Rapids
Toqua

BLUE EARTH
Cambria
Decoria
Eagle Lake
Garden City
Good Thunder
Judson
Lake Crystal

Lincoln
Lyra
Madison Lake
Mankato
McPherson
Medo
Minneopa
Rapidan
South Bend
Vernon Center

BROWN
Bashaw
Comfrey
Eden
Hanska
Home
Iberia
Leavenworth
New Ulm
North Star
Sigel
Sleepy Eye
Springfield

CARLTON
Black Hoof
Cloquet
Esko
Kalevala
Kettle River
Moose Lake
Nemadji
Net
Scanlon
Thomson
Venoah

Wrenshall
Wright

CARVER
Benton
Chanhassen
Chaska
Cologne
Coney Island
Dahlgren
Götaholm
Hamburg
Laketown
New Germany
Victoria
Waconia
Watertown
Young America

CASS
Ah-Gwah-Ching
Backus
Bena
Boy Lake
Boy River
Bull Moose
Bungo
Byron
Cuba
Cyphers
Deerfield
Gull
Hackensack
Leech Lake
Lima
May
McKinley

Mildred
Mud Lake
Nushka
Outing
Pike Bay
    (see Pike)
Pillager
Remer
Schley
Shingobee
Smoky Hollow
Sylvan
Trelipe
Turtle Lake
Wabedo
Walden
Walker
Winnibigoshish
Woodrow

CHIPPEWA
Clara City
Crate
Gluek
Granite Falls
Havelock
Lone Tree
Maynard
Milan
Montevideo
Mooseville
Sparta

CHISAGO
Almelund
Branch
Center City

Comfort
Franconia
Lindstrom
North Branch
Rush
Rushseba
St. Croix
Stark
Sunrise
Taylors Falls
Wyoming

CLAY
Alliance
Averill
Barnesville
Comstock
Dilworth
Eglon
Felton
Flowing
Georgetown
Glyndon
Hawley
Holy Cross
Kragnes
Moorhead
Parke
Red

CLEARWATER
Bagley
Bear
Beard
Eddy
Four-legged
Gonvick

Itasca
Little Chicago
Little Man Trap
    (see Mantrap)
Minerva
Popple
Shevlin
Sibilant
Willborg

COOK
Abita
Carlton Peak
Cascade
Colville
Devil Track
Diarrhoea
Eagle
Flour
Grand Marais
Grand Portage
Greenwood (see
    Diarrhoea)
Hovland
Hungry Jack
Lutsen
Mesabi
Pigeon
Saganaga
Sawtooth
Superior
Tofte
Vermilion

COTTONWOOD
Bingham Lake
Carson

Delft
Dutch Charley's
Hurricane
Kemi
Midway
Mountain Lake
Rose Hill
Windom

CROW WING
Baxter
Brainerd
Breezy Point
Crosby
Cuyuna
Davenport
Emily
Fort Ripley
Ironton (see
    Klondike)
Klondike
Lake Hubert
Long Lake
Nisswa
Nokay Lake
Pelican
Pequot Lakes
Roosevelt
Sibley
Swanburg
Watertown

DAKOTA
Apple Valley
Black Dog
Burnsville
Castle Rock

Douglas
Eagan
Eureka
Farmington
Hastings
Inver Grove
    Heights
Lake Marion
Lakeville
Mendota
Pike
Ravenna
Rosemount
South St. Paul
Vermillion (see
    Vermilion)
Wescott

DODGE
Berne
Canisteo
Dodge Center
Ellington
Hayfield
Kasson
Mantorville
Sacramento
Vernon (see Ver-
    non Center)
Wasioja

DOUGLAS
Alexandria
Carlos
Evansville
Forada
Garfield

Irene
Kensington
La Grand
Lake Mary
Miltona
Nelson
Orange
Osakis

FARIBAULT
Barber
Blue Earth
Clark
Delavan
Elmore
Foster
Frost
Grapeland
Guckeen
Jo Daviess
Kiester
Minnesota
    Lake (see
        Minnesota)
Pilot Grove
Verona
Wells
Winnebago

FILLMORE
Amherst
Bratsberg
Canton
Carimona
Carrolton
Chatfield
Cherry Grove

Chickentown
Chimney Rock
Clear Grit
Eagle Rocks
Etna
Fountain
Harmony
Jordan
Lanesboro
Lime City
Lost
Mystery Cave
Preston
Root
Rushford
Spring Valley
Stringtown
Sumner

FREEBORN
Albert Lea
Bancroft
Bath
Carlston
Conger
Hartland
Hollandale
Knatvold
Moscow
Nunda

GOODHUE
Barn Bluff
Cannon Falls
Cherry Grove
Frontenac
Kenyon

Lake City
Minneola
Pepin
Pine Island
Prairie Island
Red Wing
Stanton
Vasa
Wacouta
Wanamingo
Welch
Wells
Zumbrota

GRANT
Barrett
Elbow Lake
Hereford
Herman
Lightning
Logan
Macsville
Mustinka
Norcross
Pomme de Terre
Worm

HENNEPIN
Bloomington
Brooklyn Center
Brooklyn Park
Calhoun
Champlin
Corcoran
Crystal
Dayton
Deephaven

Eden Prairie
Edina
Excelsior
Golden Valley
Greenfield
Harriet
Hassan
Hopkins
Independence
Loretto
Maple Grove
Maple Plain
Medicine Lake
Medina
Minneapolis
Minnehaha Falls
Minnetonka
Minnetrista
Mound
New Hope
Orono
Osseo
Plymouth
Richfield
Robbinsdale
Rockford
St. Anthony
St. Bonifacius
St. Louis Park
Shingle
Shorewood
Snelling
Wayzata

HOUSTON
Black Hammer
Caledonia

Hokah
La Crescent
Looneyville
Money Creek
Root
Sheldon
Target
Winnebago
Yucatan

HUBBARD
Akeley
Arago
Badoura
Kabekona
Lake Alice
Laporte
Mantrap
Nevis
Park Rapids
Plantagenet
Schoolcraft
Steamboat

ISANTI
Athens
Bradford
Cambridge
Dalbo
North Branch
Oxford
Rum
Spectacle
Stanchfield
Walbo
Wyanett

ITASCA
Ball Club
Bowstring
Calumet
Cohasset
Coleraine
Cowhorn
Cut Foot
    Sioux
Dewey
Effie
Franklin
Good Hope
Grand Rapids
Greenway
Harris
Keewatin
Long Lake
Marble
Mesabi
Nashwauk
Nowhere
Oteneagen
Pokegama
Sago
Siseebakwet
Snowball
Suomi
Taconite
Togo
Vermilion
Warba
Wawina

JACKSON
Heron Lake
Independence

La Crosse
Miloma
Minneota
Okabena
Petersburg
Weimer
Wilder

KANABEC
Ann Lake
Arthur
Brunswick
Coin
Comfort
Ford
Groundhouse
Knife Lake
Mora
Peace
Quamba
Warman
Whited

KANDIYOHI
Bertha
Blomkest
Colfax
Dovre
Fahlun
Florida
Foot
Gennessee
Green Lake
Irving
Lake Lillian
Mamre
New London

Pay
Prinsburg
Regal
Spicer
Svea
Willmar

KITTSON
Beaton
Hallock
Hill
Karlstad
Lake Bronson
McKinley
Poppleton
   (see Popple)
Red
St. Joseph
Svea
Tegner

KOOCHICHING
Bannock
Bridgie
Dentaybow
Dinner Creek
Happyland
International
   Falls
Lindford
Manitou
Mizpah
Rainy
Rat Root
Sturgeon River
   (see Sturgeon
   Lake)

Summerville
Williams

LAC QUI PARLE
Agassiz
Arena
Baxter
Bellingham
Camp Release
Cerro Gordo
Dawson
Freeland
Garfield
Madison
Manfred
Perry
Yellow Bank

LAKE
Beaver Bay
Castle Danger
Fall Lake
Finland
Gooseberry
Isabella
Kawishiwi
Knife River
Little Marais
Manitou
Mesabi
Nigger Hill
Silver Bay
Splitrock
Superior
Two Harbors
Vermilion

**LAKE OF THE
   WOODS**
Angle
Baudette
Carp
Eugene
Le Claire
Northwest Angle
Penasse
Peppermint
Rainy
Roosevelt
Spooner
Wabanica
Walhalla
Williams
Winter Road
Zippel

LE SUEUR
Cleveland
Derrynane
Elysian
Kasota
Kilkenny
Lanesburg
Le Center
Montgomery
New Prague
Ottawa
Washington
Waterville

LINCOLN
Alta Vista
Arco
Danebod

Dead Coon (see
    Coon Creek)
Ivanhoe
Lake Benton
Marble
Marshfield
Verdi
Wilno

LYON
Balaton
Coon Creek
Cottonwood
Custer
Ghent
Lynd
Marshall
Minneota
Sigel
Tracy
Vallers

MAHNOMEN
Beaulieu
Bejou
Chief
Nay-tah-waush
Pembina
Popple Grove
    (see Popple)
Tulaby
    (see Trelipe)
Waubun

MARSHALL
Alvarado
Argyle

Comstock
Donnelly
Excel
Florian
Grygla
Lincoln
New Folden
Newfolden
Oslo
Radium
Red
Stephen
Vega
Veldt
Viking
Warren

MARTIN
Burnt Out
Ceylon
Dunnell
Fairmont
Granada
Imogene
Lake Belt
Lake Fremont
Manyaska
Sherburn
Silver Lake
Tenhassen
Trimont
Truman
Welcome

MCLEOD
Acoma
Brownton

Buffalo
Glencoe
Hale
Hook
Hutchinson
Silver Lake
Sumter
Winsted

MEEKER
Acton
Corvuso
Cosmos
Dassel
Eden Valley
Ellsworth
Litchfield
Ripley
Strout
Union Grove
Watkins

MILLE LACS
Battle
Bogus Brook
Brickton
Fogg
Greenbush
Kathio
Milaca
Onamia
Pease
Princeton
Rum
Vineland
Wahkon

MORRISON
Belle Prairie
Bowlus
Buh
Clough
Darling
Fort Ripley
Freedhem
Hillman
Little Falls
Pierz
Pike Creek
   (see Pike)
Pulaski
Rail Prairie
Royalton
Sobieski
Upsala

MOWER
Adams
Austin
Grand Meadow
Lansing
Lodi
Marshall
Nevada
Red Rock
Root
Sargeant
Taopi
Udolpho

MURRAY
Avoca
Belfast
Chanarambie

Currie
Des Moines River
Fulda
Holly
Shetek
Slayton

NICOLLET
Belgrade
Bernadotte
Lafayette
Ridgely
St. Peter
Scandia Grove
   (see Scandia)
Traverse
West Newton

NOBLES
Adrian
Dundee
Ellsworth
Graham Lakes
Kinbrae
Leota
Reading
Rushmore
Willmont
Worthington

NORMAN
Ada
Borup
Gary
Good Hope
Hendrum
Home Lake

Lake Ida
Red
Rolette
Strand
Waukon

OLMSTED
Bear
Byron
Cascade
Chatfield
Doty
Eyota
Farmington
Judge
Laird
Marion
Oronoco
Rochester
Root
Stewartville
Viola

OTTER TAIL
Amor
Battle
Clitherall
Dead Lake
Dent
Eastern
Fergus Falls
Henning
Leaf Mountain
Maplewood
Molly Stark
New York Mills
Oscar

Pelican
Pelican Rapids
Perham
Richdale
Richville
Rothsay
St. Olaf
Topelius
Tumuli
Vergas
Western

PENNINGTON
Goodridge
Hazel
Hickory
St. Hilaire
Silverton
Star
Thief River Falls
Tweet
Wyandotte

PINE
Askov
Banning
Beroun
Bruno
Chengwatana
Crosby
Grindstone
Hinckley
Kettle River
Milburn
Munch
Norman
Partridge

Pokegama
Royalton
St. Croix
Sandstone
Sturgeon Lake
Windemere

PIPESTONE
Cazenovia
Eden
Edgerton
Grange
Hatfield
Jasper
Rock
Sweet
Troy

POLK
Andover
Arthur
Badger
Beltrami
Brooten
Climax
Crookston
East Grand Forks
Eden
Eldred
Euclid
Fertile
Fisher
Fosston
Garfield
Gentilly
Hubbard
Key West

Keystone
King
Mentor
Queen
Red
Rosebud
Vineland

POPE
Ben Wade
Farwell
Gilchrist
Glenwood
Langhei
Minnewaska
Reno
Starbuck
Swenoda
Villard
Walden
White Bear Lake

RAMSEY
Arden Hills
Battle
Falcon Heights
Kaposia
    (see Battle)
Lauderdale
Little Canada
Maplewood
Mounds View
New Brighton
North Oaks
North St. Paul
Pig's Eye
Reserve

Riverview (see
   West St. Paul)
Rose
Roseville
St. Anthony Park
St. Paul
Shoreview
Spring Lake Park
Vadnais Heights
West St. Paul
White Bear
White Bear Lake

RED LAKE
Dorothy
Garnes
Grit
Lambert
Oklee
Plummer
Red Lake Falls
Terrebonne
Wylie

REDWOOD
Johnsonville
Lamberton
Lucan
Milroy
North Hero
Ramsey
Redwood Falls
Revere
Rowena
Sanborn
Seaforth
Wabasso

Walnut Grove
Wanda

RENVILLE
Birch Cooley
Bird Island
Buffalo Lake
Fairfax
Flora
Franklin
Hector
Olivia
Osceola
Palmyra
Sacred Heart
Troy

RICE
Dundas
Erin
Faribault
Mazaska
Morristown
Nerstrand
Northfield
Shieldsville
Veseli
Wells

ROCK
Ash Creek
Beaver Creek
Hills
Jasper
Kenneth
Luverne
Martin

Mound
Rose Dell
Steen

ROSEAU
Badger
Dewey
Eddy
Falun
Greenbush
Lake
Lake of the
   Woods
Leo
Lind
Roosevelt
Salol
Strathcona
Warroad

ST. LOUIS
Arbutus
Artichoke
Aurora
Babbitt
Biwabik
Buhl
Canosia
Chisholm
Cook
Duluth
Ely
Embarrass
Esquagama
Eveleth
Floodwood
Fond du Lac

Gilbert
Grand Lake
Great Scott
Herman
Hibbing
Hoyt Lakes
Kabetogama
La Croix
Lucknow
McKinley
Mountain
    Iron
Nagonab
Oneota
Partridge
Pike
Proctor
Rainy
Sandy
Seven Beaver
Soudan
Stuntz
Superior
Tower
Vermillion
    (see Vermilion)
Virginia
Voyageurs
Wakemup

SCOTT
Belle Plaine
Blakeley
Cedar Lake
Credit River
Jackson

Jordan
New Market
New Prague
Prior Lake
Savage
Shakopee
Spring Lake

SHERBURNE
Baldwin
Battle
Becker
Big Lake
Elk River
Haven
Livonia
Orrock
Palmer
Princeton
Reformatory
Rum
St. Cloud
Santiago
Zimmerman

SIBLEY
Arlington
Bismarck
Cornish
Dryden
Gaylord
Gibbon
Henderson
Jessenland
Kelso
Moltke

Transit
Winthrop

STEARNS
Albany
Avon
Belgrade
Brockway
Brooten
Cold Spring
Collegeville
Eden Valley
Fair Haven
Freeport
Holding
Holdingford
Le Sauk (see Sauk
    Rapids)
Melrose
Paynesville
Richmond
St. Augusta
St. Cloud
St. Joseph
St. Wendel
Sartell
Sauk (see
    Sauk Rapids)
Sauk Centre
Waite Park
Wakefield

STEELE
Aurora
Bixby
Blooming Prairie

Ellendale
Havana
Litomysl
Medford
Merton
Owatonna
Somerset

STEVENS
Chokio
Darnen
Donnelly
Everglade
Hancock
Hodges
Morris
Potosi
Sahlinark
Synnes

SWIFT
Appleton
Benson
Clontarf
Edison
Hassel
Kerkhoven
Pillsbury
Swenoda
Tara

TODD
Bertha
Browerville
Clarissa
Clotho
Eagle Bend

Grey Eagle
Kandota
Long Prairie
Osakis
Pillsbury
Sauk (see Sauk
    Rapids)
Staples
Villard

TRAVERSE
Browns Valley
Croke
Dollymont
Maudada
Tara
Tintah
Wheaton

WABASHA
Conception
Hyde Park
Lake City
Mazeppa
Minneiska
Pepin
Plainview
Reads Landing
Tepeeota
Zumbro
Zumbro Falls

WADENA
Blueberry
Cat
Menahga
Nimrod

Red Eye
Sebeka
Shell City
Shell River
Verndale

WASECA
Blooming Grove
Byron
Iosco
Janesville
Lilly (see Lily)
Lily
Okaman (see
    Okabena)
Vista
Waterlynn
Woodville

WASHINGTON
Afton
Bayport
Copas
Cottage Grove
Forest Lake
Grant
Grey Cloud
    Island
Hugo
Lake Elmo
Mahtomedi
May
Medicine Wood
Newport
Oak Park Heights
Oakdale
Red Rock

St. Croix
St. Paul Park
Scandia
Stillwater
Willernie
Woodbury

WATONWAN
Butterfield
Darfur
Echols
Godahl
Kansas
Lewisville
Long Lake
Madelia
Odin
St. James
Sveadahl

WILKIN
Bradford
Breckenridge
Doran
Nashua
Prairie View

Red
Rothsay
Whiskey
Wolverton

WINONA
The Arches
Bethany
Dakota
Elba
Goodview
Minneiska
Nodine
Richmond
Rollingstone
St. Charles
Witoka

WRIGHT
Annandale
Buffalo
Clearwater
Cokato
Corinna
Delano
Franklin

French Lake
Hasty
Howard Lake
Maple Lake
Marysville
Monticello
Otsego
Pulaski
Rockford
St. Michael
Silver Creek
Waverly
Winneshiek

YELLOW
MEDICINE
Burr
Canby
Florida
Granite Falls
Hazel Run
Norman
Porter
St. Leo
Stavanger
Tyro

JOIN THE MINNESOTA HISTORICAL SOCIETY TODAY! IT'S THE BEST DEAL IN HISTORY!

The Minnesota Historical Society is the nation's premier state historical society. Founded in 1849, the Society collects, preserves, and tells the story of Minnesota's past through innovative museum exhibits, extensive collections and libraries, educational programs, historic sites, and book and magazine publishing. Membership support is vital to the Society's ability to serve its ever-broadening and increasingly diverse public with programs and services that are educational, engaging, and entertaining.

What are the benefits of membership?

Members enjoy:
- a subscription to the quarterly magazine *Minnesota History;*
- *Member News* newsletter and events calendar;
- Unlimited free admission to the Society's 25 historic sites;
- Discounts on purchases from MHS Press, and on other purchases and services in our museum stores, library, Café Minnesota, and much more;
- Reciprocal benefits at more than 70 historical organizations and museums in over 40 states through Time Travelers;
- Satisfaction of knowing your membership helps support the Society's programs.

Membership fees/categories:
- $55 Household (2 adults and children under 18 in same household)
- $50 Senior Household (age 65+ for 2 adults)
- $45 Individual (1 adult)
- $40 Senior Individual (age 65+ for 1 adult)
- $100 Associate
- $250 Contributing
- $500 Sustaining
- $1,000 North Star Circle

Join by phone or email. To order by phone, call 651/296-0332 (TTY 651/282-6073) or e-mail membership@mnhs.org. Benefits extend one year from date of joining.